It's A Man's Work That's Never Done, Not A Woman's

To all who are lovers of truth and each other, and who remember consistency is the key to any breakthrough with loyalty, honesty and wanting the best for others.

It's A Man's Work That's Never Done, Not A Woman's

Written By
Shirley A. Jones

Cover ClipArt By
Open Clipart-Vectors

Interior Image By
Mohamed Hassan

Full Cover Created By
Sun Child Wind Spirit

Proofread By
Mylia Tiye Mal Jaza

It's A Man's Work That's Never Done, Not A Woman's
Copyright © 2019, Shirley A. Jones
All Rights Reserved.
Series, Volume 1

ISBN-13: 978-1703848069

This art is a book of non-fiction. No part of this work may be reproduced or transmitted in any form or by any means (graphic, electronic, magnetic, photographic, or mechanical - including photocopying, recording, taping, or by any information storage/retrieval system) without the written permission of the author/publisher. Post demise of author/publisher, then valid permission for reproduction and transmittal must be obtained from multiple immediate/major survivors of the author's family. Although careful preparation of this work permeated every phase, it is understood that perfection is humanly impossible. Further, the content of this book does not serve as professional counseling. Thus, neither the self-publishing associate, author/publisher nor imprinter accepts liability for errors, omissions, nor damages resulting from the use of any information presented herein.

<u>Author</u>
Shirley A. Jones
shirleyjones339@gmail.com
www.ShirleyJones.webs.com

<u>Self-Publishing Associate</u>
Dr. Mary M. Jefferson
BePublished.Org - Chicago, IL
(972) 880-8316
www.bepublished.org

First Edition. Printed In the USA
Recycled Paper Encouraged.

Table of Content

Acknowledgements 135

The Art & Artist 137

Chapter 1: The Way It Is 9
    A Poem 14

Chapter 2: Rimmne & Zypporah's Big Day 18

Chapter 3: Herald and Darsha 53

Chapter 4: Franklin and Náyai 77

CHAPTER 1
The Way It Is

It's believed that a woman's work is never done. For many years, this has been the way most of the world saw relationships and marriages. Because we're creatures of habit, it's easy to fall into a trend or a pattern when it comes to what, when, who, how and why things happen to us or in our lives. We mostly judge things by what we see and what's tangible, not the things unseen.

Clichés that stick are like a volcano that has erupted. There's no reset button. It's all over the place, wrecking and tearing down anything that's on or in its path. And, what was is no longer the same. It's often mentioned by women how their desire is for men to commit, be loyal, caring, to be gallantry (show chivalry) and remain truthful. And of course, the million-dollar cliché: "Happy life, happy wife."

Now ask yourself these questions: Who are you depending on to make your life happy? Who are you depending on to protect you and keep you safe? Who are you beholding to make sure there's stability and security in your marriage? Can a woman do these things by herself, on her own?

Of course, she can! But, when she's married, these titles are transferred over to HIM. Don't misconstrue what I'm saying. But, if the things you have for him to do as a husband, friend, lover, father etc., supersede what you have for yourself, then whose work is never done?

Yes, some of you may say, "God is who and where my strength lies. He is who I depend on to keep me safe and covered."

Then, I ask, why did you ask for a husband? What purpose does he serve in your life? Why was your prayer answered? Let me help you out. It's because the life journey you desire and feel you deserve, you can't get it done alone (here on the earth's soil); and, when you get hit and knocked down by the whirlwinds of life and feel like you're at the end of your proverbial rope and you now believe more will be put on you than you feel you can bear, you're going to need and or want close proximity natural physical assistance.

Let me share a few HOT OFF THE PRESS life-changing pointers The Father taught me about "He who findeth a wife findeth a good thing and his favor." This is what He taught me: It's okay for a woman to let a man know she's interested in getting to know him. Now, I know that this is a big no-no to many who believe that a man should make the first move, because it's been taught and said over a hundred billion times that "she should let him approach her, come for her, and take it from there."

What if he's pre-occupied (mentally)? What if he's thinking on how he can get his company to the next level or any other life-changing successful thoughts he may be having? So, he's not paying attention to, or seeing, you or anyone else. Should he miss out on a wonderful, good looking, kind-hearted, caring woman as yourself just because he's thinking about what he should be prioritizing at that moment and time?

I hear you saying, "Well, it wasn't meant to be."

Okay then, miss out on possibly the best opportunity you'll have in years to come because of an antiquated cliché. Well, for the Christians, let me ask you this: Have you ever heard a woman say she started to go to one store but something steered or told her to go to another one and that's where she meet her husband?

Or, "I kept running into the same man. For weeks, he keep showing up where I was. So, I asked in a joking manner, 'Are you following me?' And a relationship started from that conversation?"

Yes, he could have been following you, but you (the woman) started the conversation. And, for those of you (women) who caught him with your body gestures – you know that walk we get when we either think he's looking or want him to notice us by playing with our hair or reaching for that product on the top shelf hoping he's paying attention and come over to help. All of these are first moves, ladies. Whether we use our words or our gestures, they're all verbs (actions).

So, my lesson was when He said, "He that findeth a wife." Was God teaching his sons that when you find a wife (not a cuddle buddy, not a common-law woman, not a casual sex partner, nor a girlfriend or even a fiancée, but a wife) you've done good? Now you know the difference. Once you make her your wife, then you find His favor.

Question: Who are we to matchbox how love is to be introduced or become acquainted with? Does that much power lie in our hands? I think not. Moving forward. Let me tell you one other lesson I learned.

If you're in a relationship or married, and you have an upcoming special event (such as an anniversary, birthday, or any other occasion), remind him that the date is approaching so you can, at least, have a chance of having a good outcome. As we know, most men (not all) forget major dates and occasions and women get furious about that. It's been this way for centuries. But, if you know he's going to forget or it slips his mind, then be that suitable helper to make memories and history of that special day. Do this instead of waiting for the setup that will only create bad memories and get your feelings and emotions out of balance, not to mention the stain it will leave on that special day.

I believe it's not in the nature of a man to remember dates of special occasions. It's not because he doesn't care, but because it's not a part of his nature – just like it's not in the nature of a woman to remember when the oil in her car needs changing or the time to rotate the tires on her car. Can it be done? Of course! But, when you go against the nature of a person, place or thing, you don't get the full potential of its purpose.

If he's the provider and the protector, can't you be the calendar? You're probably going to go where you desire anyway. So, why not make good memories? If you'll remind him that you're going shopping, on a cruise with the girls, out to celebrate a friend's birthday, or to your company's party, why not remind him of the special occasions? Is it not more important? The choice is yours.

A POEM
(06/21/1998)

A Father will never leave you
in the midst of a euroclydon storm
Just like Jesus will never forsake you
and keep you from all harm

He's the head of his family
As Christ is of the church
It's found in 1st Corinthians 11:3
So, there's no need to search

A father has to stand, give, and take
some things that he may not like
But in the end God will prevail
so, pray for him day and night

A father's thoughts of responsibilities
Are mostly in his head

And almost never spoken out loud
But the necessary things are said

If there's a special occasion
that you feel he should always know
Don't wait anxiously to test/trap his memory
Remember, what you've reaped is what you've sown

A Father is a man who cares
About the things that are unseen
Because the things unseen is eternal
That's what the BIBLE reads

So, if you're sitting next to a father
Give him a genuine hug
Because he need to hear and know
That he's appreciated and loved

A father has a special way of loving you
And making everything (or most) ok
He's never too busy to show his love
So, fathers, thank you and
HAPPY FATHER'S DAY!

Sometimes, a man has to step outside of himself to see the mistakes he's made or is making in order to be able to change his ways – or, at least, better his actions and thoughts. If you haven't noticed, things that bother women don't necessary bother men. This too has been the case for many centuries. If he loves you, it's because of what he sees in you and what he desires in a woman that you possess. It is NOT for what we (woman) mostly think we have to have to catch and keep him.

For example: You feel you have to be shaped like a fake / pseudo / false / feminist woman and have long, flowing hair (added or grown). When, in fact, he married you because you cook very well and your heart is kind. Or, you feel that the way to get the best out of a man is to be a great cook, but he married you because you do more listening and help solve issues than judging and taking over the conversation – of course, the cooking is always a bonus. Or, you thought that, if you showed him you were independent and drive a top of the line vehicle (which is okay), that he would prefer you. But, for him it was your lady-like persona and family values.

So, you get it right? Know the why about how he sought / choose or was led to you and married you. Once you know the why, then you will understand what it is about you that keeps him attracted to you, what he loves about you, and vice versa. Most of my young adulthood life, I heard, "God gave women a female intuition that men don't have." So, we really have an advantage on them. Most men don't say, "I had a feeling she was seeing somebody else," verses women saying (even before they have proof of infidelity or disloyalty), "I know it" or "I felt he was doing something."

Growing up in the sixties we heard that "two heads are better than one." And now, it's three heads are better than two and a fresh set of eyes wouldn't hurt because, sooner or later, we find ourselves entangled in web-weaved ropes of life and lay self-decisions at the feet of our mate or others to possibly justify our actions. In your reading, you will see another side of responsibilities and the lap it rests in.

If you're still reading, then I've piqued your interest. If you let go of your premeditative thoughts, we can board the cruise ship of "Whose Work Is Never Done." Now, let's get into the three different types of men with three different types of responsibilities and scenarios.

CHAPTER 2
Rimmne & Zypporah's Big Day

The big day was here! It was Rimmne and Herald's graduation from DMWU (Dad and Mom Wings University). After four years of high school and 4-6 more of college, they felt ready to take on the ways and the weight of the world. It was time for them to become the men their parents taught them to be – responsible, loving, hardworking, focused, successful and frugal with their finances. Their parents were doing the best they could to prepare their sons for life. Now, it was hands off and hats on.

"And now I present to you for the first time, Mr. & Mrs. Dr. Rimmne & Zypporah Amwind."

The sun was in favor of Rimmne and Zypporah's special day. It shined upon the earth so, until they felt nothing could spoil their wedding day. They vowed to always communicate with one another and respect and listen with an open mind to each other's point of view before responding.

After the ceremony, Zypporah decided that a cruise to the Caribbean would be the best honeymoon ever. It was what she wanted and the life most women could only dream of, the wife of a doctor and a home in the Hamptons.

Dr. Rimmne G. Amwind, MD (GP), he thought to himself, *I did it. A licensed doctor and married my high school sweetheart. What more could a man ask for, other than little blessings from God, children?*

Little did Rimmne know, his life was just beginning. The position of a husband and being a father are two different roles in life. The honeymoon wasn't over. After a week of rest, it was time to start their new life together as husband and wife.

After a long day of seeing patients, Rimmne would rush home and wrap his arms around his wife. He would kiss and love on her, and thank her for agreeing to be his wife and the mother of the three children they both agreed on. This was how their life was for several months, until one day, during the wintery months.

Zypporah had a special dinner fixed by the time her husband got home. She decided to tell him through dessert that he would be a father soon. After dinner, she brought out his favorite dessert, swirl ice cream in a covered sterling silver bowl nicely centered on a saucer. After his third scoop, he found a pacifier in the middle of his ice cream. With the look of ultimate surprise and gratefulness, he stumbled through the words of a first-time father to be.

"Does this mean what I think it means"?

And with a huge Kool-Aid smile rested on her face, she answers, "CONGRATULATION, daddy in seven months!"

In a matter of seconds, Rimmne found himself on his knees with his head in her lap and his arms wrapped around her tummy. He was rejoicing through silent tears. Their first baby was on the way, and life as they knew it was about to change again. School, love, happiness, marriage and family were the desires of their hearts.

Being a homemaker by choice, Zypporah had her own line of jewelry. She also designed her own wedding ring, a 27-carat double diamond wedding set with five rows of diamonds, amethyst, sapphires and rubies. Diamonds for her husband, rubies for her, sapphires for her two boys, and amethyst for their daughter. They prayed for children in that order of gender.

Before long, the time had come and the newest member of the family was ready to be present and accounted for.

Rimmne was at work when he got the page that his wife was in labor and headed to the hospital. He had just started to examine a patient and, as a courtesy to the patient, he didn't look at his pager.

Zypporah was prepped and ready to deliver. But, she was a little stressed and concerned that her husband wouldn't make it in time. He promised he would be there at every birth. Worrying caused her blood pressure to rise and she was rushed down to the delivery room. What she didn't know was that her husband was already scrubbed in, waiting for her at the doors. As they approached the delivery room doors, she heard his voice telling her to open her eyes.

"I'm here, babe, relax. I wouldn't miss this for anything in the world."

Once she saw his face, she exhaled sending her blood pressure back to a safe and normal rate.

"He's here, Rimmne Gerald Amwind Jr." the doctor said. "Seven pounds and three ounces."

After a few days of recovery, they were home starting their new life as parents. Zypporah was still a little weak, so she was surprised with two temporary live-in nurses – one for her and a neonatal nurse for RJ. Rimmne had to get back to work, but not before he made sure his family was well taken care of while he was away.

His responsibility had increased tremendously, with Zypporah on bed rest. The proud father of a new baby boy had to step up his game and still be there for his patients. As a daily routine, he'd call home to talk to RJ on speakerphone, making sure he knew daddy loved him. Then, he'd finish his rounds at work and go home to his family, and do it all over again the next day.

Rimmne soon hired gardeners to keep the grounds and make sure they trimmed the hedges just like Zypporah liked them. Her preference was one set of hedges shaped in rows of five hearts, each heart represented the family they planned to have. The rest of the grounds was for normal keeping.

Rimmne decided to make the neonatal nurse position permanent. It was easier for Zypporah and he wouldn't have to be as concern about everything running smooth at the house while he worked and attended to other needs of the family. Every night after a long day's work, he made sure to give his family his undivided attention and not talk about problems or issues from work – unless she asked or if it was a major change for the family.

The honeymoon still wasn't over, Rimmne continued to court and date his wife and surprise her with unexpected gifts. Love making was essential for the both of them. They promised to never let life's curves or their differences in opinion enter their bedroom. All disagreements and problem discussions that needed to be hashed out were taken to the den or the "Lovefrontational Room" (as opposed to confrontational) and they talked there. Any unresolved issues were left in that room until the next day or agreed upon time to resolve it.

Rimmne remembered the wise words from his parents. His mother's words were to never go to bed angry and never take arguments and anger into the bedroom.

"It's a leach that will suck the life out of your relationship and marriage."

But, his father's words were sharp, swift and to the point.

"Anything you feed will live and grow, and anything you starve will eventually die."

It has been a little over two years since the grand opening of GBBH (Good Better Best Health). The patient clientele has increased, and it was time to look for a larger place or modify the one he was in to save money and prepare for their second baby by the end of the year. Even though it may cost him more money than he wanted to spend, moving into a larger building would be easier for him and less inconvenience for his patients with little to no construction.

On his way home, thinking about the major changes of the clinic, Rimmne knew he had to run these developments by his wife. If there's one thing a man has realized, it is never make a major change or decision without talking to the wife. *Happy wife, happy life*, he thought. Having heard that saying a thousand times while growing up, he always thought that statement was a bit one-sided and unfair.

A wise older patient told him one day, "The life of a happy wife is because the husband is making life nice."

Now, that's what Rimmne thinks every time he hears someone make that statement.

"Babe, I'm home," Rimmne shouts as he enters the home through the garage doors.

"Okay, I'll be right down," Zypporah said.

"I need to talk to you about my thoughts on increasing the clinic."

"Okay, give me a minute to put RJ to bed and we'll talk over dinner,"

"Okay, honey. I'll wash up and meet you in the dining room."

Ten minutes later, they were eating and discussing whether to add on or move to another location.

"I think we should just modify the building," says Zypporah. "Save money and make the patients as comfortable as possible during the construction. Plus, I don't want to move. I love our home. Please, baby, think about it."

Rimmne said, "Okay, I will. Now, can we call it a night? I think the both of you need my attention.

He smiles with all 32 showing,

"I'm not sure about the little one, but I always need your attention, husband of mine," Zypporah said.

And, with a kiss, Rimmne carries her upstairs to shower and have a little pillow talk before sleep. Honoring his wife's request, he decided to modify the clinic and have human resources to setup interviews for more employees and to bring on a Family Practitioner.

After months of construction, the clinic was finished and back in stride again. Everything was working out fine. The wife is happy, patients were pleased and impressed and getting heathier, and Rimmne saved money. The only concern was that Zypporah seemed to be picking up more weight than usual with this pregnancy.

"She's been eating more but, I guess, it's to be expected. Every pregnancy is different and, then too, we are hoping for another boy this time and then later my little angel of a daughter."

Just like a couple in love, they tend to think alike and feel each other's vibes and thoughts. Zypporah had a doctor's appointment. She only had a few months left before delivery. She too had noticed that her weight was a bit more than it was with RJ and the baby, for the last few months, had been very active. Rimmne and RJ would talk, play and read to the baby almost every day but it seemed that, after all the commotion was over, the baby would start up again and it was hard to rest during the evening.

"I'll mention it to Dr. Farquhar and see what he thinks, I'm a bit tired and slower this pregnancy. I think I may be overdoing it. I'd better take it easy a let Tramayne mind the jewelry store while I rest and get off my feet," Zypporah said.

To Zypporah, Dr. Farquhar was the best doctor ever, with the exception of her husband, who is the best in the world. Dr. Farquhar wanted to ease Zypporah's concerns, so he did a sonogram of the baby. For some reason, he started to display a strange expression on his face. After the false scare with her in-laws Darsha and Herald, Zypporah was afraid something was wrong.

"What is it, doc? You're starting to scare me," she expressed.

"Oh, no worries, Mrs. Amwind. Everything is fine. As a matter of fact, we have an unexpected guest," Dr. Farquhar said.

"An unexpected guest? I don't understand," Zypporah said.

Before he could answer, it hit her. The extra weight gain. The tiredness and being slower than normal.

"Dr. Farquhar, am I having twins?"

"Give me a minute and I'll be able to confirm that. Can you roll slightly toward me?"

"Sure, I think."

With the greatest effort, Zypporah rolls slowly toward the doctor.

"There, hold it right there," he said. "Well, I'll be John Henry Brown. Yes, Mrs. Amwind, I can confirm that you're carrying two babies,"

"OH MY, GOD! Two?"

"Yes, two," Dr. Farquhar said.

"Can you tell the sex?" Zypporah asked.

"I'm not sure, but I can try. How did we miss the second baby? Well, she was hiding behind her brother."

Tears begin to run down Zypporah's face.

"Twins! A girl and a boy?"

"Yes, ma'am, you have one of each. Would you like a printout of them?"

"Yes, please. It'll help tell their father he's a hardworking man in more ways than one."

"Okie dokie. Here's your delightful surprise. Sorry about that. Usually two sacs are easy to spot, but since you've had such a healthy pregnancy, the unexpected wasn't a concern until they became very playful and heavy."

"Well, I'll start seeing you every week now."

"I want to keep an eye on the little one. She's a lot smaller than I'd like, but everything looks fine. Go home and get lots of rest, you're going to need it these last weeks."

Zypporah was a little nervous and excited. She had to find a way to break the news to Rimmne that his daughter was coming a lot sooner than planned, accompanying her twin brother. When the day had ended, Rimmne remembered he needed to stop by the auto shop and get the car summarized and make an appointment for Zypporah's car to be done the next day. While he was taking care of the car business, Zypporah was having a hard time trying to come up with a way to tell her husband about the babies.

She thought about calling her mother- in-law and asking her how she told Daddy Herrim they were having twins, but then she decided against it because she wanted Rimmne to be the first to know about the babies before anyone else. Zypporah decided to call her mom for help on how to tell Rimmne the extra weight gain was his daughter. Besides, who better to talk to than your mom about life changing situations and surprises for your hubby, lover and best friend.

CHECK POINT

MONEY doesn't free A MAN from his RESPONSIBILITIES.

Just because a man is rich or wealthy (and there is a difference), it doesn't mean his responsibilities ease up or go away. Yes, having money makes life easier if you handle it right. But, responsibilities are like land and air. They're everywhere and there's no escaping it as long as you're above ground.

Scenario 1

He's living a comfortable life with butlers, maids and gardeners to keep life for he and his family as comfortable as desired. But, he still must know the needs of his family, what must be done, and how it needs to be done. He has to know who can get the job done right the first time around without wasting his money. It's imperative for him to identify who's capable of keeping his family safe and protected in his absence.

You don't leave your family's fate in the hands of people you pay without instructions regarding "The Dos & Don'ts" for your household. It's his responsibility to make sure every helper is capable, reliable, dependable, and can and will follow instructions explicitly.

Now if you're caught up in the "help" aka servants, then you're missing the point. They're servants by choice. People who choose to help others in any capacity see it as a blessing for them to help and they love what they do. It isn't embarrassing nor something they're ashamed of. It is what they consider to be a way of life.

Who are we to minimize and tear down what they consider a gift and or an honest living? I realize things and opportunities are available now that haven't been in years. But, to utilize them too is a choice. Let's move on to another scenario.

Scenario 2

He's a hardworking family man with a wife and three children living well above poverty. A five-figure salary and punching a clock, he has a nanny but no maids or butlers. Still, life is comfortable and durable. The children are in private schools and his wife works also, but she's having a hard time on the job and comes home frustrated most of the time. He catches the heat because she's wanting to be a stay-at-home mom and wants him to release the nanny from charge.

They've discussed it, but he had skepticism that this was the best plan for his family. What if some unfortunate accident or injury seals his fate and he's no longer able to work, how would the family be taken care of with the both of them not working? How would it work if she had no job but had to be the sole financial provider for the family? Yes, it happens all the time. But, what's forgotten is that a man who's used to handling his business, sweating by his brows as it says in the Bible for a man to do to take care of his family, finds it very difficult not being able to be the backbone and provider.

Yes, there are some who find it okay and, if it works for their family and it can't be helped, then that's a wonderful thing. But ALL men have egos. And, no matter what hand fate has allocated to them, the ego isn't budging. Stroke it or fight it, but please understand it's not going anywhere. It's a built-in apparatus from the beginning of time. Women are considered nurturers by nature, so if you want a loving, consenting life and / or marriage, let the head of your household do his job.

And, here's a nugget for you: If he's the head, then you're the neck. Every head needs a neck to

> connect it to the body to function properly. That's how life is durable and grand. His responsibility is to not only take care of his family now, but he has to plan for the future also.

After talking to her mother, Zypporah decided she would break the news during a night of passionate loving making. She knew that, after the babies, it would be a while before she's able to give herself to him like that again. She had dinner ready and Nurse Jones had put RJ to bed and retired herself for the night as requested. Rimmne got home later than usual and they had dinner and prepared for bed. They showered together and headed to retire for the night.

Rimmne, being tired from an exhausting day, kissed his wife goodnight and turned over to go to sleep. Zypporah initiated the love making and, of course, Rimmne complied. With such little time left, it didn't matter. He never rejects her when she desires him.

Starting at her toes and working his way up, he felt a strange cluster of something he couldn't figure out. So, he pulled back the covers and saw an amethyst and powder blue bow, one on each side of the entry way, and thought they were going to play a new game she'd come up with. He had no idea what their purpose was and why he was stopped at the doorway of great pleasure. He raised up. Sitting on bending knees, he asked her what the next move was.

With a smile of uncertainty, she told him the ribbons were the results of a hardworking man who's great at everything he does, "To the second power."

It took him a minute to figure out what she meant, silence fell over the room, Rimmne got out of bed leaving her stunt and wondering where in the world was he going and what was going on in his mind. He returned with a purple box and repositioned himself between her thighs. This time, the look was more familiar. He was smiling and nervous. He opened the box and removed a 7-carat amethyst (emerald cut) diamond ring and placed it on her right hand.

He kissed it and said, "That's for giving me a daughter and going through everything it takes to carry and give birth to her, increasing our family."

She smiled and chuckled a little.

"What's got you so amused?" he asked.

"What about the blue ribbon?"

"RJ is already here, baby. His little sister is just coming a little ahead of schedule."

"Not really," she said.

"What do you mean?" He said, looking puzzled and confused.

"Your daughter will be accompanying her brother. We're having twins. That's what the blue ribbon is for, daddy," Zypporah said and fell back in a rage of laughter at the look on his face.

"Two babies?"

"Yes, Dr. Feelgood, two babies."

Now they both were laughing at the fact that he was slow in getting the gist of the two ribbons. Once the element of surprise was over, they celebrated the good news by finishing her request to be made love to. And, Rimmne was more than happy enough to comply, while feeling there's nothing like your hard work being appreciated and wanted. Everybody was nurtured.

Just to inform you, as a reader of my book, let me educate you a little about two different sacs (babies). This means that Zypporah was impregnated twice. Two sacs, each with a boy and a girl, are fertilized by two separate sperms. Look it up. It's a medical fact. Fraternal twins make Rimmne a bad boy in my opinion.

Boy, oh boy. What a night that was! Rimmne was thinking to himself while Zypporah was resting peacefully. With the two new additions on the way, there was much to be done for Dr. Feelgood (in the words of Zypporah). Instead of the baby girl having a room of her own amethyst and pink, she'll be sharing a room of amethyst and powder blue with her brother.

I know Zypporah will not want to separate the twins too soon, if at all. So, they'll be sharing a room together. The twin's nursery was the room closest to theirs and RJ's so they could better monitor them when Nurse Jones was off.

"Oh my, God!" Rimmne thought out loud.

What will we name them? In a panic, he rushed into his bedroom to alert Zypporah, only to find her sitting up with a list of names for them to consider for the twins.

"I should have known you'd have a list ready," Rimmne said, crawling back into bed beside her to take a look at the list of names. "I love you so much."

He gave her a soft kiss on the lips.

"And I love you more," she replied. "Now, let's get down to business."

He started to caress and kiss her breasts while his hands were making their way down the between her thighs.

"What are you doing?" She giggled a little.

"Getting down to business."

Through her laughter, she pops his hand and said, "Not that business. I'm talking about the names for the twin's silly."

He said, "Oh, tell me something, baby. I thought you wanted an encore of that standing ovation from last night," and he laughs.

"Oh, don't worry," she says. "I'll be needing that encore again tonight. The time is closer and soon you'll be on lockdown. It drives me crazy not being able to have my Dr. Feelgood morning, noon and or night."

They both laugh. After their long deliberation, Zanae Diamond and Zyon Demear would be the twins' names.

"Now that we've gotten that settled, the nursery is next."

It only took a few days to get the twins nursey finished. Instead of amethyst, they incorporated lavender and powder blue with teddy bears, ABC blocks, and choo-choo trains. Not long after everything was ready and in place, the twins were ready to make their debut. Once again, Dr. Amwind's pager went off while he was with a patient but, he was able to tag team with the new physician, Dr. Xerra Knocking-Boots. She had become very familiar with his patients and had a pretty good clientele herself.

Most of Dr. Boots patients followed her to GBBH and all new patients that didn't request Dr. Amwind went to her. Rimmne explained to his patient that he was getting ready to be a father for the second time but to twins this time around. His patient being seen that day, expecting herself, was very understanding. He asked her to allow Dr. Boots to finish her checkup while he went to be with his wife for the birth of their babies.

The patient agreed. And, as promised, Rimmne was there at the beginning of the twin's delivery. But, there were complication with Zanae. Zyon was delivered at 5lbs and 3oz, but Zanae was smaller and stuck. The umbilical cord was wrapped around her neck and Zypporah wasn't fully dilated. Dr. Farquhar had to move quickly.

He told Zypporah to push, hoping that would force her daughter down the canal but it didn't work. So, he had to take drastic measures. He explained to mom and dad what needed to be done to get Zanae out and they agreed. Dr. Farquhar pushed on Zypporah's stomach, forcing the baby down the canal. She stopped shy of Zypporah's vaginal opening. Dr. Farquhar was able to remove the cord from around her neck.

Zypporah was frantic and Rimmne was praying that his baby girl would follow in the footsteps of her brother and be okay. Knowing, as a doctor, the issues she could have from the cord being around her neck, he was also concerned that she was a little underweight. Regardless of how nervous and worried

Rimmne was, he knew the one thing he had to do was to keep his wife's blood pressure from skyrocketing by being in control himself and being strong for them both.

Finally, it was over. Zanae was born, but she was a blue color. That meant her oxygen was cut off for a certain amount of time and she needed immediate attention. She weighed 3lbs and 7oz and it worked out for her good. She was small but not critical. The nurses moved expeditiously to check her vitals to see if there were any issues that needed immediate attention.

Zypporah lost it. Neither one of them being able to hold her was heart-wrenching. Zypporah's vitals escalated, and she started to hyperventilate. Rimmne told the nurses that were cleaning up Zyon to give him to his mother. He knew that was the only thing at the time that would get his wife's vitals back to normal. Once the baby was in her arms, she settled for a bit. When Zyon begin to cry, her motherly nurturing kicked in and she began to pacify him. That took her mind off Zanae just long enough for her to get him comforted.

While trying to remain calm and not lose it for the health of his wife, Rimmne's heart was breaking from not knowing what was going on with his little princess. He was drowning in his own hidden tears. Just as the tears welled in his eyes while standing at the head of the delivery bed, a nurse walked through the doors with Zanae in her bed and a small tube coming from her mouth.

"To ease her breathing until she was at least five pounds or she can breathe on her own without help," the nurse quickly explained. "Everything else is fine."

After a few weeks in the hospital, Zanae had gained enough weight for her family to take her home. When Rimmne and his family pulled up, their relatives were there to welcome them home. Both moms had packed bags and they planned to stay a while to help out with the babies and take care of Zypporah and RJ until Zypporah was able to get back on her feet.

When Rimmne returned to work, his employees and colleague had gifts and cards to congratulate him on the newest arrivals to the family. He and Zypporah decided to have brunch at the house for the employees so they could meet the children and give their gifts before returning back to work after an extended lunch break. Even after weeks had passed, they were still talking about how beautiful the house was and how precious the babies were and the love and unity Dr. Amwind and his wife shared as a couple.

CHECK POINT

Please understand, when it came to the health and welfare of his family (life and or death), his money couldn't do a daggone thing. It had no relevance, place nor power. It couldn't take the umbilical cord from around his baby girl's neck. It couldn't reverse the vital signs of a worried mother, and it couldn't hold back tears of a wealthy doctor, husband and father who had a baby in trouble. Yes, it's good to have but, just remember, there are a lot of things money can't buy now or ever.

Rimmne had to hold back his emotions and fears because his family was in a crisis and his wife's health was in danger of failing. Society says, "Happy wife, happy life." But, I beg to differ. If Rimmne, as the head of the family and a doctor, would have broken down – and he had every right to be greatly concerned and fearful for his wife and daughter – Zypporah's reactions would have tripled his. Because as a wife, if your husband can't see a way through or out of your present situation, then life as you knew it would no longer be the same. Stability comes into question, leadership comes into question, and his capability would be challenged.

And, I will say this to those of you who will possibly say, "I would have done" this and "I would have done" that because "Nothing would have kept me from" doing whatever. Making whomever your him is feel incapable, weak, dismissed, worthless is all because most have been taught or heard, "Don't depend on a man. Make it happen yourself. Real men don't cry. Sometimes you have to wear the pants," and so on and so on.

Questions

If you do step into the pants, when does he get them back, and how long before you step into them again?

I've heard and talked to women who wanted their men to be hard and protective but when they're having their crying moments, what part of this hard and protective man do you desire to hold you and comfort you?

Just like women say to men, "I'm not a toy to be played with," well, aren't you expecting him to be a slinky or a teeter totter?

Don't you cry, but hold me when I do. Don't try to tell me what to do, but protect me at all costs, Really?

It's not a competition. All men are not alike. They don't all have dogmatic ways and animalistic behaviors. All men are not the way they are by choice. If there was no mentoring, fathering, or a realistic hero in their lives to lead and guide them to and through manhood, then how do they obtain this knowledge the right way?

I say to women who feel they have to step in the pants of their men: What was it about him that made you say, "Okay, I will," or "I do." Did you see through the window of possibilities like the spirit of Isaac's wife Rebekah when she used her wits to get her way once he went blind (or, nowadays, didn't agree with you)? Or, was it the heart of Delilah, work it / him until you're in control and he's then no good for you or anyone else?

I promise you, I'm not throwing stones because I too lived in a glasshouse until I built it with bricks. If you had a granny like I did, then you too have been told, "You get as good as you give and sometimes more if you use honey." Treat your husband in such a way that he will not only protect you and your honor, but he will trust you with his whole heart.

If you've ever been in a relationship with a man, then you know that's not easy for some men to do. Now, if you're asking or saying, "What about women? Men have been doing this and doing that since the beginning of time!" These are my questions for you:

Was what he was doing at the beginning of time available for you? Is it available now? Have you heard of any women doing it nowadays? Or, are you just now realizing you have choices too, you matter too, you have a voice too?

Don't lose your dignity, love and comfortable life just to be right or in control. Take a poll of your friends who are in control of their man and wears the pants. Ask her if she would show up at a prestige black-tie government event on his arm. If he were asked to speak on unity or relationships, what would he say about the relationship he's in with you? If he spoke on how to let your woman wear the pants so life at home could be peaceful, what would he be wearing at this black-tie event? An A-line skirt of yours with designer support pantyhose and a top that coordinates with his pants you're wearing?

I will say this: What happens in the dark will soon find its way to the light. Or, you know that washer and dryer cliché, so choose your battles. Don't lose yourself in shoulda-woulda-coulda's and control. Is winning worth it? The choice is yours.

It has been a year now since the birth of the twins and RJ is now three. Zypporah is back on her feet and her mom and mother-in-law have gone back home. They hated to leave the babies, but they knew their husbands were in need of their nurturing, love, care and attention. Besides, it had been a few months, and all was well with the children. So, their parents left looking forward to the family visiting soon. Things were back to normal. Well, as normal as it could be with a three-year-old and a set of one-year-old twins getting into any and everything that was on their path.

Not wanting to add on to the care of the children by Nurse Jones (who was doing a great job helping with the babies), Zypporah decided to work from home and promote Tramayne to manager since she'd done such a great job both times Zypporah was out on maternity leave. There were no problems, which meant the jewelry store was one thing she didn't have to worry about. That was a big relief. Knowing how difficult it could be running the store alone, Tramayne was able to hire an assistant.

It was winter and the holidays were right around the corner. The store was very busy, and the sales excelled when Zypporah decided to design a limited edition line of baby rings named after her and Rimmne's children. A sapphire with three diamonds was called RJ. The sapphire with two diamonds on opposite sides was named for Zyon. And, an amethyst made in the shape of a heart with baguettes was called the Zanae. Each customer could have their child's name engraved on the inside of the ring free of charge if they desired to do. But, the baby rings were only for the holidays. They were personal and memorable to customers as well.

Things were starting to get a little rough for Rimmne. The clinic was extremely busy and, with the change of weather, the clientele increased greatly. So much so until they weren't leaving work until hours past closing. That changed things at the house, causing a bit of friction between he and the wife. Zypporah was used to Rimmne coming home like clockwork and helping with the babies after having dinner together. With the new doctor on board, she figured, no matter how busy it got, Dr. Boots could handle the overflow.

Rimmne didn't see it that way. It was his duty as chief physician and CEO to make sure the clinic ran as smooth as possible, with decency and respect to the patients and to Dr. Boots. Leaving her there to weather the storm of patients alone was unfair and unethical, and that wasn't the kind of doctor or boss Rimmne was.

On the late nights he would get home from work, he would make sure to give extra attention to Zypporah. He was hoping to keep alive the spark they had between them as lovers, best-friends and as spouses. He didn't take for granted that her work at home was any easier than it was at the store. The differences were the people at the store were customers and mostly strangers. But, the people that were with her daily were her babies and that's personal – more attention, more love, more action, and more work. Rimmne remembered what his father told him when it came to women and what they deed was right.

His father told him, "Only bend as far as your spine will allow you because, if it snaps then you're no good for her nor yourself. A man's spine is considered his back representing his action, to brake it could result in death or being permanently paralyze, so the stronger his back is the more pressure he can carry and the more weight he can hold upon his shoulders.

"You see, son, once a man bends over backward for the love of his life -- and not all do or have to -- making sure her desires and wants are taken care of and a little extra for the surprised nurse outfit on occasions for the grown and sexy extra curriculum activity, when the elasticity of his back returns him right-side-up his love and actions should be reciprocated. He should encounter respect and gratitude. He should be seen in a different perspective It should prove to her that he's willing to do what it takes for happiness and being on one accord to keep love, peace, hope, joy and unity in the marriage and or relationship."

While trying to keep his home running as normal as possible, Rimmne encountered a personal matter at work. One night, after a long strand of patients and walk ins, he and Dr. Boots ended up in the breakroom for a cup of coffee and cocoa for Rimmne. They sat down to rest their minds and their feet and started to talk about how well the clinic was running and how pleased the patients seemed to be even at the end of a long visit.

Dr. Boots changed the conversation and began to praise Rimmne for such a wonderful family and a beautiful home. Not being loquacious on the subject, he said, "Thank you," and proceeded to get up and leave. That's when he met face-to-face with Dr. Boots, where she attempted to kiss him.

Questions

What will he do?

What should he do?

Is your relationship strong enough for him to walk away?

Is he so undressed because you're wearing the pants until he's looking for an attire of a consistent lady?

Did he leave home hungry and, now that work has prolonged his coming home, will the fast food that's offered be his appetizer and/or his meal?

When your garden is out of lettuce, is there and option available for him to troll into another garden, or do you have a substitute dish that's just as good if not better in place of what's not available?

Are you so stern when he's home until there's no room for compromising – so much so that the smallest submission elsewhere is appealing?

What would the man in your life do?

STAY TUNED . . .

CHAPTER 3
Herald and Darsha

Herald was the CEO of Amwind Oil & Gas, and the family's lawyer. Being married wasn't high on his list of priorities, at least not at this time in his life. He knew one day he would want a woman by his side to share his life with and maybe a child to carry on his bequest, an offspring to pass the baton to. But, for now, a girlfriend was all he could manage. That's why Darsha was a part of his life. Darsha met Herald during her first year of law school. He was on his way out, but not before making her his lady. She's the love in his life and has been for three years now.

Her final year in law school had finally come. As she prepared for the bar exam, she started to daydream about the life desires she's had since she was a little girl. Now, those dreams were on the horizon. She dreamed of having her own firm, "Darsha Blackkard Law Firm." They both had dreams, desires and goals. With determination, prayer and family support, they both eventually succeeded.

After four years strong into their relationship things began to change. Herald started to feel the squeeze from Darsha to take their relationship to the next level. They both had very demanding careers and he felt their status was find the way it was. But, being raised by parents who taught him all about commitment and how not to allow work to consume him so much, Herald knew he didn't want to miss out on God's precious gifts of life, love, marriage and family if desired.

He thought about it and decided to not prolong the inevitable. So, he planned a surprise engagement party and wedding to propose in a way that was unforgettable. He called her father and asked for his daughter's hand in marriage. After he got her father's blessing, he invited all of their family and friends to their surprise engagement and wedding ceremony. Herald figured, *Why wait to plan another event, when it could be done all at once?* And the icing on the cake was his flying Darsha's best friend in from Ireland to sing their favorite song; "I Do Believe That God Above Created You For Me To Love" by S.A. Jones.

Darsha had no idea of all Herald had planned. After Uacesa's flight got in, she was rushed to the ballroom to set up the second part of the surprise. The first part of the surprise was

Darsha's associates had gathered to celebrate the biggest case her firm had won so far. Everyone cleared the floor while Herald and Darsha shared an intimate dance of victory. At the end of the song, he dropped down on one knee and proposed.

With tears of joy, she said, "YES!"

And, he placed a three-carat platinum marquise diamond ring surrounded with baguettes on her finger. Then, he stood tall, leaned in, and saluted her with a kiss.

"It's only just begun," he whispered. "I have another surprise for you."

When she turned toward the curtains hanging behind the stage, Uacesa walked out. Darsha was too shocked to move. Uacesa ran over and embraced her. Even though they occasionally talk on the phone, it had been years since they've actually seen one another. Darsha turns and look at her future husband and blows him a kiss of thanks. The night was still young, and the final curtains hadn't been drawn. After everything in the back was ready, it was time for the biggest surprise ever.

Uacesa was a seamstress. She brought a wedding dress and told Darsha she wanted her opinion on it. She asked her to try it on and model it for the guests to see if they thought it was "beautiful enough for the Queen of England." Darsha was honored. She changed into the cancan and the white gown covered in double rows of rhinestones down the train with a cluster of stones covering the front of a heart-shaped strapless bodice. Uacesa placed a tiara on Darsha's head.

Darsha realized it was the gown she had chosen years ago for the grand opening of Uacesa's store. It opened with a smash. Uacesa had a few friend girls to model some dresses she designed. And, Darsha choose the "Queen of England" dress to model when she walked the runway. Darsha felt as though she was a princess in a fairytale about to marry her prince.

Uacesa had instructed her to come out once she was ready, and that she did. Having just gotten engaged to the man she can't see herself living without – her best-friend, her lover – and now she's wearing a beautiful gown that was to live forever for (not to die for), this was a night she would never forget. Darsha was ready. She walked down the corridor that lead to the opening of the ballroom. There to greet her at the door was her father. With a smile of surprise on her face, Darsha's father took her by the arm and escorted her to a red-carpet runner that lead up the aisle to her waiting prince.

When Darsha realized what was happening, she stopped and grabbed her heart. She gasped for her breath. Her feet wouldn't move. Her father released her arm as she began to scan the room. She saw the faces of her family and friends, and Herald standing at a built altar with their minister.

Herald took one look at her and saw the better part of himself. He felt overwhelming love. He was nervous and proud at the same time. The surprise for him was he'd never seen the dress and how stunning Darsha looked in it.

He asked her with trembling words, "Would you agree to marry me now, right here today?"

Darsha slowly shook her head and whispered yes, but she was still in shock and her feet wouldn't move. Herald held his hand out for her to come to him and she didn't move. Realizing she too was overwhelmed, he walked towards her after softly whispering, "Baby, I'm coming."

As he got closer, her knees started to buckle so he carried her cradled in his arms back down to the altar. Her father followed behind them to announce his giving her away. It was almost too good to be true. Darsha was marring the man of her dreams, the man whose life was so busy until she didn't think he would land long enough to get married. She definitely didn't think he had these kinds of skills to plan such a wonderful engagement and wedding surprise.

"I now pronounce you husband and wife," said Minister Johnson.

Herald and Darsha's life pretty much remained the same for three years, until she became ill and had to be admitted into the hospital. Herald was out of town on business when he got the news. He took the first thing moving back home. When the plane landed, he hit the ground running to get to her. A thousand things ran through his mind as he wondered what could be wrong. *There's no way I'm losing my wife*, he thought. He began to talk to the Lord.

"Lord, you gave me the woman of my hopes and dreams. Please let her be alright," he prayed. "I love her, and I need her Lord."

Herald begin to reflect back on the day his mother got sick and his father was right there by her side until she was discharged and back at home with him, where she belonged. By the time he arrived and located her, Darsha was asleep in her room. She left specific instructions with the nurses not to tell her husband what was going on with her condition. She wanted to be the one to explain it to him herself.

After a few hours of sleep, she awoke to her husband lying wrapped around her like a bow on a present. She turned over and stared into a pair of loving and nervous hazel eyes. She laid her hand on his face and told him not to worry, that everything was okay, and they would work through their situation together. Tears welled in Darsha's big brown eyes.

"What situation babe? Tell me what's wrong."

Sitting up in the bed, Darsha wiped away her fallen tears. She wondered how he was going to feel about becoming a father at this time in their life. The oil and gas company had taken on as many clients as it could handle. Darsha's firm had been in the news for the last two years for winning three more of the most public and controversial cases their town had ever seen. Her firm was now booked for the next 18 months.

Herald joined her and sat up. He pressured her to tell him what was going on.

"Honey, our lives are so busy right now with traveling and long hours. Is there any more room on our plates for anyone else?" Darsha asked.

"Anyone else? Babe, I don't understand," Herald said.

She politely picked his hand up and laid it slightly beneath her breast while looking at him with great concern.

"What is it?" *Is there something wrong with the girl's breast?* He wondered.

She shook her head, "No."

Darsha moved Herald's hand a little farther down her abdomen and pressed his hand to her stomach. He still didn't get it. He thought she had gas. So, she called to the nurse's station and requested that there be no more visitors for the day. She said she just wanted to spend the rest of the night with her husband undisturbed.

After a nurse came in and all of her vitals were taken, her request was granted. Darsha wasn't due to be discharged until the next morning. That gave her plenty of time to break the news to her husband. Being in a private room on the floor with only three other patients, she decided to tell him in a way most men understand and are able to be relaxed after the fact.

After getting him to calm down, they took a nice shower and she promised to tell him all about her hospital visit once they were in bed. Herald did feel a little better knowing that his wife didn't have a life-threatening situation that would take her away from him. After very little coercing, and I mean very little, she managed to give him what she felt he needed to relax.

He felt like he had just hit the lottery of love. Then, she placed his left hand between her legs. She slowly slid it up to her stomach again. Then, he got it. He jumped up from the bed slowly and weak. He turned on the bedside light.

Stumbling over his words again, "Are you telling me, for the second time in my life, you're making me one of the happiest men ever?"

"Are you really happy?" Darsha asked. "I thought, with our schedules being so unbalanced, that you wouldn't be ready for a baby right now."

"Yes, our schedules are hectic but, through it all, we created a life. This is a sign telling us it's time to stop focusing so much on our careers and enjoy the fruits of our labor," he said.

"Then, you're happy that we're having a baby?"

"Yes, yes, yes, I'm happy. I can't wait to tell dad and mom that they're about to be grandparents again."

Darsha was relaxed and happy that business as usual would no longer be the same. After they were home and rested they began planning for three now that a baby was on the way. Six months to be exact. Work had to take a back seat. Colleagues, foreman and partners had to keep the balls rolling while life changed their courses of action.

Herald called his parents and gave them the good news. He also needed to talk to his father about the responsibility of being a new dad. He knew it would happen sooner or later, but he wanted to be mentally "daddy" prepared. He was nervous and excited, and in need of a little father and son pow-wow. Herald even considered calling his twin, since he's on his way to be a father for the second time. *Surely, he could shine some light on what it's like.*

Their father, Herrim, decided to take his boys where his father took him when it was time for a man-to-man reality talk. They went to Lake Kewon and sat on the dock of the bay.

"Sons, life and children don't come with a manual. You experience them both one day at a time, with future plans and patience. Society missed it. Just because most men don't interact in their children's lives, that doesn't speak for all men. The blinders society has on the eyes of people, mostly women, put men in a pool of unconcern and none nurturing. No, we don't have what a woman has to physically nurture a baby. But, we can be a visual and communitive helper to them both.

"What I'm saying is change your baby's diaper and talk to them. That's where familiarity starts. Hold and caress them. Let them feel your strength and love. Look into their little faces and let them see their father, the man who's going to protect them with every fiber of his being and assure them, to the best of his ability, that everything is going to be okay.

"When they get older, things between you may change a bit but, just know, their destination has nothing to do with who you are as their father," Herrim continued. "I'm saying, if they stray from the path, it doesn't mean you're a bad father. You can only take them so far and then you have to let go and always pray for them. See, the mother carries the child for months. That's an unbreakable bond during that time. But, when she has given birth to your blessing, you move in position to make sure your wife and child are covered, protected, safe, provided for, and loved.

"Remember you're not just held responsible by your family. There're the grandparents on both sides and, most of all, the one who holds the Lamb's Book of Life and knows all. Don't only be a father, be a friend with boundaries and an advisor with vision because the child you raise will one day be a product of their rearing. So, monitor the people you allow in their life because influences, good or bad, has a way of attaching itself and changing the course of life.

"There's no guarantee that all you've taught will be used. But the one thing you will know, if they ever have to rely on what they were taught, it's in there and they can utilize it at will. Expect the best and pray for the best, but never leave your family uncovered," Herrim said. "I'll leave you both with this. I was taught that your genitals don't make you a man, it only identifies you as a male, and fathering a child doesn't make you a father, raising them does.

"If you don't raise them, then you're considered as a donor – like men who go to the sperm bank and make a deposit for cash and wants to remain anonymous. A man takes care of the family and respects women who give birth to their children. Whether she's your wife or you missed what I taught you and made her a baby mama, either way, a father raises his own children at all cost.

"Sons, never call a WOMAN your girlfriend, because most men tend to get that mixed up. It simply means that's how you view her. A friend girl and whatever title you put on that relationship is how you will treat it. A woman will and can eventually become your wife, but a girlfriend will cater to your unstable ways and only accommodate you in the present without equity for the future. We as men have to be cautious with the title we place on our relationships. It can cause a lifetime of misery, thorns and rocks."

While Darsha was at home preparing dinner, she began to have labor pains. Though they agreed to slow down on work, Herald figured if anybody was going to keep the family covered and keep the money coming in it would be him. So, he continued to keep his workload but made a few modifications. No overtime, no out of town trips – unless super urgent, and his cell phone has to be attached to his hip at least until the baby was born.

Darsha's contractions were only a few minutes apart. As instructed, she called the doctor to put her on notice and possibly prepare for delivery should their daughter decide to make her presence known sooner rather than later. Darsha found out they were having daddy's little pineapple a month ago. Herald wanted a girl but decided he would wait and be surprised at the birth to know what the gender was.

Secretly, Darsha bought baby clothes and kept them at her mother's home. Her mom was ecstatic about her first grandbaby and the fact that it was a girl. The baby's furniture was also stored at her parent's home because it was taffy pink and pine green, which was a dead giveaway that she was carrying their "Pineapple Princess."

The name, Pineapple Princess, came from our vacation trip to Honolulu. Herald had a drink that had a pineapple and a parasol. The pineapple was so bright and yellow it remined us of the sunshine. The statement he made alerted me that my husband wanted a Pineapple Princess to love and spoil, daddy's little girl.

I guess I shouldn't be surprised. He has an ego the side of Mount Rushmore times four. History could read J. Washington, T. Jefferson, T. Roosevelt, A. Lincoln and H. Amwind for sure. She would definitely be his ego stoker right behind her mom. Herald deserves it and he has, and is continuing to, earn it. He works hard, makes good money and finishes everything he starts.

It was time for daddy's little Pineapple Princess to make her entry. Darsha was in her home office going over some of the firm's paperwork when she dilated to seven centimeters. Though the hospital was just a few miles up the street, Darsha was cutting it mighty close.

Just a few more minutes, she thought, *and I will call Herald and tell him to meet me at the hospital.* Her pain tolerance was pretty high, so she gambled a little with her labor dilation. Herald was dealing with a customer and just about to wrap up a deal to head home for the day. Seeing how Darsha could go in labor any day or time now, he didn't want to miss the birth of his baby.

Darsha was still in the office when she started to get unbearable pain and called her doctor to inform her she was on her way in. Darsha confessed that the pain was greater, and she couldn't tell how far she had dilated. She attempted to call Herald, but it was too late. The baby was coming, and fast.

Darsha called for the ambulance. She feared even they wouldn't make it before the baby would crown. So, she called Dr. Yancey and put her on speakerphone. Dr. Yancey started instructing Darsha on what to do and what she was going to need.

"First, unlock the door for the paramedics," Dr. Yancey said.

Then, she called Herald. He was already in route. Dr. Yancey advised Darsha to find a comfortable place where she could recline, and Darsha positioned herself on the chaise lounge chair. She also put a mirror at the foot of the chaise and prepared to deliver the baby by herself. Within seconds, it was time to push.

Darsha suddenly felt so foolish for waiting so long before going to the hospital. Now, the fate of her baby was left in the hands of her and Dr. Yancey – who was now video chatting with Darsha through her laptop. Tears started to fall because Darsha deeply didn't want to deliver without Herald being present. She hadn't gotten the chance to call him in time, so he was about to miss the birth of his Pineapple Princess all because of misplaced priorities.

Herald and the paramedics arrived at the same time. The baby's shoulders were out and Darsha was on the final push. Out she came as Herald and the paramedics rushed through the door. After they arrived, Dr. Yancey told Darsha she did good and she would see her soon. Once the baby was cleaned and stable, she was handed to her father. But, they had to get them both to the hospital to be checked out.

Being a little disappointed at not being there for the actual birth of his Pineapple Princess, he was very grateful that they both was okay and healthy. One of his greatest desires had favored him. Yet, he couldn't help acknowledging his feelings.

How could she be so thoughtless? He thought to himself, *She knew the one thing I wanted was to be there with her and for her, and experience the miracle of life being birthed. I wanted to be the second face my daughter saw coming into a world, where every moment she would need and deserve my love, protection, guidance and nurturing.*

Having missed an irreversible moment that can never be repeated, Herald had to focus on the fact that they both were healthy and well. He had to accept that life isn't all you want it to be and you have to make the best of every curve ball it throws at you. Just know, you don't have to swing at every pitch.

It was now time to name their little princess. Herald and Darsha decided on Pinnelope Alohi. The name is Hawaiian. It means shining and brilliant.

"Princess Amwind. A name fit for a miracle," Herald said.

After they were discharged from the hospital, both sets of grandparents were there waiting to welcome the newest addition to the family. Her room was tropical with yellow, green, orange and pink – reminding her parents of the place she was conceived.

Herald was so excited, he didn't want to hand her to anyone, but he did. Once the excitement was over, his parents stayed overnight and left the next morning. Mr. Jim and Geneva, Darsha's parents, stayed the entire week. Then, her father had to go back for work. Her mother had prepared to stay to help her until the end of the month. She was glad to have her mother there to help out.

Darsha also needed some advice on how to deal with how things turned out concerning the birth of Alohi, considering that Herald was not there due to Darsha's misplaced priorities. After she finished breast feeding the baby, Darsha and her mom had a chance to talk. Herald was downstairs in his office on the phone bragging on his Pineapple Princess to a colleague right after talking to his dad and brother. Darsha told her mom what happened and how she felt it was her fault that Herald missed Alohi's birth, and the second face she saw wasn't her father's.

"Well," her mother said, with that teachable moment look on her face, "You can't erase the past baby, but you can try to make moving forward better. First, don't allow it to fester. Find a time where the both of you are uninterrupted and apologize. Ask what he needs to move forward.

"Most of the time, men will brush it off and put it behind them. But, you can't be sure unless you hear them say everything is okay, followed by a short sentence. Most men don't talk much about their hurt feelings. If he says it's all good and nothing else then, more than likely, he's harboring it. Ask questions. But, be careful not to push too hard or make it sound like you're talking to a child. It's insulting.

"If he tells you after your talk that everything's fine, followed by a sign of relief and saying how he feels, then tells you not to worry, believe him. It is. Men just want to be respected, loved and trusted – in that order. Society focuses on women and children, leaving the men to fend for themselves when it comes to emotions, children, how to love you, and remembering special dates and times.

"So, my darling daughter, do that and make sure you include him in things you do for the baby," Darsha's mother advised. "We women tend to say, 'my baby' and not 'our baby.' I believe that comes from the old cliché, 'Mommy's baby, Daddy's maybe.' When will we, as a people, learn the opinion of others about our lives is just that, an opinion? Take it or leave it. THE CHOICE IS YOURS!"

Darsha replied, "Thanks, Mom, for always being there and helping me to realize you're never too seasoned to learn more. I so appreciate you for teaching me that knowledge is power and, without it, you're limited in all areas of your life."

After a few weeks of healing from the delivery, Darsha decided to talk to her husband so they could move forward together on one accord, or at least know what he was thinking and how he felt. She looked all over the house for him. She thought to herself, *if he's not in bed with me or in his office there's only one place he could be.* She knew actually where to find him.

"Yes," in Pinnelope's room, he was just sitting there watching her sleep. "Honey, can we talk? I need to make sure we're okay."

"Babe, what do you mean make sure we're okay? You just gave me one of the most precious gifts ever! Every time I look at her, I'm looking in the mirror. Yes. We're better than okay."

"That's great to hear, but I took something from you that can't be given back," Darsha admitted. "I was so busy with work stuff, I didn't realize that our baby could make such a quick drop. During my dilation, the pain was manageable and I felt I had more time before dilating to 10. Our instructor said, even if we dilate to a seven, it could still take hours."

"She also said it could take minutes," Herald said with a stern look on his face.

"I'm so sorry, honey," Darsha said. "I don't know how to make it up to you for missing the one thing you so desired to experience, the birth of our baby girl."

Darsha was mindful to use the word "ours" and not "my."

"Yes, I have to say it was very disappointing. But, I love you and, after seeing what you had to go through to get our princess here, there's no way I would allow my being disappointed get in the way of our future and the life we're building together," Herald confessed. "It's okay, babe. We're good."

That night's conversation was a relief for Darsha. It brought a new level of maturity for Herald. *Now that I am a father, I have to level up*, he thought while lying beside the one woman he vowed too love, cherish and protect until death parted them. And I'll add one more: FORGIVE.

NEWS FLASH

The more you spend on something, the more you value it!

Understand that habits will get in the way of what we say we value most – people, places, things, occasions, etc. If you value something or someone, you tend to treat it differently from the norm. If you owned a Bentley and a BMW and only had a one-car garage, which of these vehicles would you park in the garage?

If you owned a 27-carat diamond ring and a 2-carat silver plated ring with baguettes of cubic zirconia, which would you wear to an amusement park and which would you put in a safe at home?

Last example: If you were in the company of a gentleman who opens doors, picks up the check for whatever, and cares about your thoughts and feelings verses a man who drives a Maserati, pushes a button to open car doors for you, speaks at you instead of to you, does not display PDA, and offers no hopes of change, which man would you rather be in the company of? Which one would you value? Value means to prioritize, recognize the higher class / position, to set apart and maintain its original potential and poise.

Darsha valued the birth of their daughter, but misplaced her priorities and learned an important lesson: Never take what you value for granted.

Does Herald have a valid point? Does he have a real reason to be disappointed?

Was Darsha wrong, or was she doing what she felt needed to be done at the time?

STAY TUNED . . .

CHAPTER 4
Franklin and Náyai

Frankie was the best friend of the twins, Rimmne and Herald. He wasn't as fortunate as they were, but he had what his mother called, "a fool's wish" or dream. He wanted to become the owner of a chain of restaurants. Having lived in the shadows of others all his life without any support of his dreams from family members was like a knife in his heart. But, it forced his willpower into full throttle.

After being told over and over again that just finishing high school was enough, his mom being in no condition or position to pay for college didn't make him give up on his dream. The chance of going to college was slim to none, so he searched through the newspapers and walked the streets searching for a job. As luck would have it, Frankie found a job working in the neighborhood grocery store.

With his dream still engraved in his cranial, he worked hard and learned everything there was about every job that was given to him. This caused him to moved up the proverbial cooperate letter. After working at the grocery store for two years, he managed to work his way up from being a stock boy to assistant manager. Things were looking up for Frankie.

Then, the store hit a rough patch. They were robbed twice, and most of the workers left the store out of fear of being robbed for a third time. Due to financial challenges, the grocery store couldn't afford security. The options for employees were to quit or work at your own risk. And, that's just what Frankie did.

He figured not taking a leap of faith and going for the life he desired and dreamed of was just as high of a risk of being a nobody. Living in poverty, off vanity, or dying without trying weren't options. So, Frankie continued to work until he was able to save an enormous amount of money that would cover his bills and cover him until he was able to reach his goal to leave and start the career he had dreamed of all of his life.

Shortly after resigning from the grocery store, Frankie started working in different restaurants to gain knowledge and get the hang of the industry. After working a year, he soon was promoted to manager over one of the most prestigious establishments in the city. His dreams were finally coming to fruition. The one thing he repeated to himself over and over again was, *I can do whatever I put my mind to as long as I'm willing to move my feet.*

Franklin's hard work had paid off. Mr. Wymey, who owned several of his own well-known restaurants, gave Frank a chance to spread his wings. Everything he needed to know, Mr. Wymey taught him. He even sent Frankie to different marketing workshops and conventions so he could learn all there was to know about being a CEO. After three years under Mr. Wymey's professional tutelage, Frankie's finances increased and he was able to move into a nice loft uptown, closer to his job. *No more public transportation!* He bought himself a nice pre-owned Silver G37 Infiniti, splurging foot loose and fancy free with his money wasn't an option. He had bigger plans, and saving his money was imperative. Becoming the CEO of his own chain of restaurants was top priority, and everything else would have to wait – even a relationship, so he thought.

Very few men like being alone, and Franklin wasn't much different. While pursuing his dream, Náyai drifted in and out of his thoughts. She was a very ambitious classmate who was almost girlfriend. She was a neighbor who returned his interest while they were in high school, but it never escalated past hellos, stares and smiles. Frankie often reminisced on the long days and nights of their youth. Then, he'd fantasize about them being together and living a life of answered prayers and dreams.

With her Bulldog mentality for reaching her career goal of being a social worker, and my Great Dane devoted willpower to be successful in this industry, we could have the best of both worlds, he thought to himself. *With loyal-love, happiness and lifetime careers, there's not much left except children. And, I'm not sure I want any.*

It was hard being raised by a single parent after the divorce, living paycheck to paycheck, barely making it from meal to meal (a decent one anyway). There's a saying I heard from a few older guys that got married and started a family. They said the quickest way to kill the romance in a relationship is to put a ring on it. True or false? It makes a man think twice before the "M" word.

Enough of daydreaming, he told himself. *Back to work. Anyway, what are the chances I'll see her after all of these years. She's probably married or got a man in her life. I've never been one of those people who had things to drop in their lap. I had to scrape, crawl, beg and borrow. And even that, sometimes, didn't* work, until I meet Mr. Wymey. Now, life for me is going to be different. This "fool's dream," in the words of my mom, is now reality on the horizon and I won't ever take it for granted. Life is what you make of it. And, while I'm thinking about it, I'm going to stop having a pity party about the conditions I was raised in and how hard it was. It's time to man up, put up, or shut up.

Digging his heels in and putting his nose to the grindstone, Frankie was now the owner of four restaurants in nine years and counting. Mr. Wymey was hands off. He stepped back and watched "a fool's dream" grow legs, feet and wings and take off. Mr. Wymey was so proud of the progress Frankie had made until he gifted him another restaurant, the one where most celebrities, athletes, doctors and CEOs come to dine with friends, family and lovers.

"I remembered," said Mr. Wymey, "How ecstatic Frank was the first time I took him to The Súanvier."

We dined and watched famous people come and go the entire evening. Waitresses were dressed in amethyst tails, white bowties, black nylons, and crop heels. The waiters were in white tails, amethyst ties, and black patent leather dress shoes. There was nothing shabby about the Súanvier restaurant. And it was now all Frankie's. With such a high demand on management down to the staff, he wondered if he was ready for the dream of his life at this level, the desire of his heart. The one thing he worked so hard for was finally being dropped in his lap.

Yes! He shouted in his mind. *Yes, I'm ready!*

Before meeting his staff, Frankie asked to read the history and file of everyone working there so when he met them he would know a little about them and how they came to work at the Súanvier. Two weeks after becoming the owner of one of the greatest restaurant's in the state, he met and became familiar with his staff. It was only a few days later that all papers were signed, making him the official owner and CEO of Súanvier.

Frankie couldn't wait to call his friends and let them know what has been going on in his life and how "a fool's dream" can and has come true. He wanted to thank the twins for always encouraging him and telling him to never give up on his dream no matter what anyone said, even those who he felt should have supported him but didn't. The final call was to his mother. Frankie told her about everything that had happened, who he was, and that he was now the owner of a chain of restaurants just as he dreamed he would be.

To no surprise, his mother didn't believe him until it was broadcasted on SylverFox News. Once it was verified and now known everywhere, she felt a twinge of excitement.

"My son! A big time CEO!"

Tears escaped the wells of her eyes. The life she lived before him wasn't the greatest, but that didn't matter to him. In spite of the lack of support and disbelief, he was going to take care his mom and move her out of that place where life was very challenging – where there was poverty, hunger and difficulty surviving; where hope was the only way to a life of ease, peace and success.

Frankie's heart was broken when his mother declined his offer to move in with him and she disappeared for weeks, then months. And now, it's been a year. He had searched for her to no avail. During his search, the twins Rimmne and Herald were on board. That was, until Frankie decided to move on with his life. He still held the hope that, one day, his mother would surface.

NEWS FLASH

This is my opinion from what I've seen on my life's journey: just because you gave birth to a baby doesn't necessarily make you a mother, no more than a man impregnating a female makes him a father.

There are two sides, and there's no difference for women just because you gave birth. What I mean is, yes men who contribute to creating life (through what God has put in place to make happen) should be responsible for providing for that child or children.

I also believe it's wrong if they don't. However, I propose that it's just as wrong for a woman to use the child as punishment to try and control a man who has moved on but still desires to be a part of their child's life and pays support. It's also wrong to mention the concern about getting married to another for fear of chaos between the two parents about his new life and or wife.

My thought is, if the child was conceived casually (or as a booty call, an oops, or even a night of just something to do), more than likely it's possible the parent(s) will conduct the raising and correspondent of this child's life as such. For example, they're prone to do things like mistreat the child or act like they can't stand to look at him/her because the child is a reminder of the other parent. In these situations, the child unfairly has to pay for your feelings your emotions and your choices.

Most things in life, we see coming and choose to avoid the warnings because we think it's something about us and our ways that will change the inevitable. We go for it, only to realize we don't have what it takes to maintain what it was we wanted. Of course, there are hundreds of different scenarios that convey this. But, let me close this thought like this: When you write your life by your actions, make sure your co-author and or producer(s) are on the same page. Consistency is the key to any breakthrough, but a divided cast crew will crash.

After such a disappointing and draining search for his mom, Frankie decided to take a short vacation to relax and rejuvenate his mind body and soul. He wanted to go somewhere that didn't demand his time nor attention beyond the norm. Hawaii had been a place of his dreams since he was a boy. But he figured, with the hand life had dealt him, there was no chance of that dream ever coming to pass.

But here he is, grown and successful, boarding a cruise ship – unbeknownst to his employees, who think it's just another normal conference – headed to another dream that has proven his childhood doubts to be wrong. A 7-days/7-nights trip is just what Frankie needed. It was time to think about what social life he wanted, and who would be brave enough to give him a chance at love and that legendary happily ever after.

The ship set sail later that Sunday evening, and Frankie was able to relax and not have to check on the restaurants or anything job related for the first time in a long time. As usual, while taking in the evening breeze, he started to reminisce about the one woman that could bring peace and serenity to all the chaos in his heart, Náyai Godlub, his high school crush.

If he never saw her again. she would always be Mrs. Franklin D. Deluvirus in his mind. *Another fool's dream*, he thought, being reminded of the words from his mother. But, it didn't take long for him to remember he's living "the fool's dream," proving that they do come to pass if you do what it takes. Frankie started to think of the responsibility that comes with a relationship and marriage. Was he ready to take on a life that requires him to be responsible for someone other than himself?

Later that night, the ship had the usual disco party on the deck. Frankie, drinking a purple voodoo, enhanced his passion to do one of things he was good at, dancing. He finished his drink and hit the deck. He danced until every worry, every issue, and every bad thought that had entered his mind was gone, at least for the moment. It was well past midnight when he decided to turn in. Before he could reach the portal of his hall entry, Eboni and Ivory stop him to asked if they could accompany him for a nightcap.

"We've been watching you do your thang all night and thought there's no way a man like you should go to bed alone so we propose you invite us in for the night," Ivory said.

"Well, ladies, I accept your proposal on one condition," he said.

"What is that?" Eboni asked.

"That you both write a note of consensual sex, open range, at will."

"Deal," they chimed in unison.

The night began and ended on a night to remember. Later that morning, Frankie couldn't believe he just had a menajahtwa. Who would have thought in a million years, even a zillion, this would or could happen to him? Not knowing if they knew who he was never crossed his mine.

NEWS FLASH

Will these ladies approach him again? What are the chances he'll get an encore two nights in a row? The one question he should ask himself is whether they know who he is and what he does for a living? Or, was he so out of it that they went through his things just to find out his name in order to Google him before they made their second move?

See, men are just as vulnerable as women. They too can be deceived (manipulated, used, hoodwinked, bamboozled) and endure all the things we think men do to women to get what they want. And, ladies, if you keep it real with yourself, just because it's not said out loud doesn't mean it isn't so. How many times have we found out his weakness and used it for our better good?

Come on now. The truth will make you feel better – that's if your goal and desire is to have a lasting, loving relationship or a long-lasting marriage. If you're a reader of The Good Book, then you know a few of the females were deceiving and misleading men a long time before men caught on. Yes, I'm saying we, as women, taught them the how to.

In Genesis Chapter 27, Isaac's wife (Rebekah) and his second son (Jacob) tricked Isaac and his first son (Ishmael) out of the inheritance intended for the first son. This was the plan of the woman taking advantage of her blind husband. This is in the Bible, ladies. So, if you want to live a life of love, peace, serenity and all that you hope and desire it to be, then be an honest, loving, suitable helper. Be a calendar for the best memories and history you've created with the man you vowed to be there with for better or worse, and everything else you said right before I Do.

Oh, I can hear the most of you saying, "What about him? Shouldn't he do the same?" Well, that depends on the kind of man you chose to say I do to. Were you in a rush because you thought he might change his mind? Then, what does that say about your relationship to come?

Were you patient and waited on him? Or, did you jump in the driver's seat, taking the wheel, and are now wondering why he's so submissive – not only to you, but all of the other women in his life as well.

The work a man has to put in to make his woman/wife pleased (happy, safe, wanting him in all ways, etc.,) is never ending. We can be very needy at times. Think about how much pressure is put on a man by his father, who's raising him to be a good man.

Consider the pressure from his mother, who's teaching him how to treat a woman. Now, think about society dictating how a man should act and how to treat not only his lady but all ladies. Top that with The Good Book that tells him to treat his wife "as Christ treated the church."

No, none of these are bad. Not at all. But, when was the first time or the last that you read any of these things to be done by a woman? Just because he's considered 99% of the time the stronger one, does he deserve less?

When a man is cheated on, deceived or used by a gold digger or what have you, then he's broken and embarrassed. He, as a man, has been misused by a woman. He, supposedly, should be more charismatic and convincing than that, according to the "Player Player's Handbook" for those who have animalistic ways and dogmatic behaviors.

There's no one particular gender accused of having these animalistic ways and dogmatic behaviors. If we stop allowing society to pick and choose our way of life, then maybe there's a chance at true love, like some have mastered already.

Now look at Frankie, who just had double pleasure for the first time ever. Was he the one with a motive? Most would say he got the better end of the deal. Well, that depends.

After a well-deserved vacation, Frankie went back to work. Business was the same as usual. The thought of his mom crossed his mind, and silent tears invaded his emotions so much it led him to the museum of his mind of fiction or future. Was the life he desired fiction or was it the future he dared to pursue? Why couldn't he have the woman of his dreams, if she's unmarried? Society has controlled his life much too long, telling men who and what is out of their league and if you're rich or wealthy, marry or be with someone of that same status.

"Keeping it in the money," they say.

From what I've observed, that doesn't work out for a lot of the rich and famous or celebrities. Instead of finding somebody to love them for them and not for what they have, it appears to be the furthest thought from their minds. Love is sometimes difficult to find without adding drama to the ingredient.

It was Humpday, and all restaurants were doing fine for except Súanvier uptown. A movie director came in with his crew and wanted to rent out the entire restaurant upon his unreserved and unscheduled arrival, which was impossible. It was the busiest time of the day and people were dinning. Frankie offered him their private Bella Ballroom upstairs that would seat him and his entire cast. There was a lot of whispering because this director and his crew were well known and were coming upon their fifth season on-air soon.

Frankie thrives on keeping all customers satisfied – movie stars, celebrities, groups or families. All who dined at Súanvier with reservations or private bookings were welcomed and accommodated when available. It was very seldom that the restaurant was too full to seat more customers. Its capacity was built to accommodate 200 guests, plus the Bella Ballroom upstairs could accommodate an additional 300.

Now that all fires were put out, Frankie decided to call it a night and head home for a little R&R. He poured himself a glass of wine and grabbed his high school yearbook to reminisce about the one girl he has loved forever. When the twins dropped by, they helped him look for his mother.

Frankie remembered coming across information about his alma mater helping low-income students with college funds, and Nayai's name was mentioned as one of the social workers. This was his opportunity to find her and hopefully the sparks they had in high school would still be there. He called the school administration office for information on the social worker, Godlub, but they had nothing.

"I have to find her," he told Herald and Rimmne. "I'm so close but, yet, so far."

The one thing that had him so nervous was that Náyai could possibly be engaged or married. After a few days had passed, he decided to check out the school's website for different programs they had going on. He was hoping to get some kind of information on Náyai. Once again, his search was a dead-end.

The wine kicked in, and it was lights out. Frankie wasn't a heavy drinker. But, he did like a good glass of wine every now and then. For him, it was a nice sedative for sweet sleep most of the time.

It was month-end and time to check the revenue of his businesses. Upstairs at Súanvier is where his main office was and his financial staff worked. Though most things are computerized and technology is on high demand, Frankie knew it was still good to keep good staff in arms reach. After all the numbers were in, reality hit him like a ton of bricks (figuratively speaking). He was a multi-millionaire!

For the last year, Frankie's focus had been on looking for his mother and his "ship in the night" lover and hopefully wife, Náyai. He didn't stop to think that all of his hard work and success would make him a millionaire so soon. Yes, he figured someday it would. *But, at the age of 27?* His family tree wasn't quite the tree of great people, not even good, so this is definitely a milestone and a first for his family.

Frankie became more determined to find his mother. But, he didn't know where to look. As a child, she would leave for hours at a time, leaving him home alone. He had no idea where she was, but she would come back with food and a little money that would last only for a few days. He didn't care to imagine the where or how. He just focused on the fact that she came back, which was more than he could say about other mothers in the neighborhood where he grew up.

Frankie decided to do what wealthy people do. He hired investigators to help him find his mother. This would give him time to realize how different his life is going to be. He went back to his old high school and, to his surprise, the same principal that was there when he and Náyai attended was still heading the school.

Frankie shared with Principal Johnson what he was doing and how successful he had become. Mr. Johnson proudly told Frankie that he had read about him in the *Sylverfox News*. He said he remembered Frankie when he saw his name "Franklin D. Deluvirus."

"I was so proud that my former student was proving that some of the young men made a decent living for themselves and a few even made it big," Mr. Johnson boasted.

As they started to reminisce about Frankie's days in high school, Mr. Johnson told him that some of his classmates came back to help other students get into college. Then, he asked Frankie if he remembered Náyai Godlub. When he mentioned her name, Frankie's heart started palpitating. *I am going to find the one and only women of my dreams!* He quickly said yes.

Mr. Johnson went on to say how Náyai was a social worker and she was working downtown, over on GTG Blvd. That was 10 minutes away from Súanvier. He thought to himself, *What a coincidence.*

"My main office is downtown as well. Maybe I'll stop by and see if there's anything I can do to help out," Frankie said.

"That would be great," Mr. Johnson responded.

"You wouldn't happen to have the address would you?" Asked Frankie.

"Why, yes. I have it right here in my rolodex," Mr. Johnson said.

He shared it with Frankie. Frankie left in a flash. Everything was working out.

"I'm wealthy! I've found the love of my life! Now, if only the investigators could find my mom, the circle would be complete for now."

NEWS FLASH

Ninety-nine percent of the time, a man will move mountains for that one true love – or, at least, that one he thinks is.

Now understand, if he goes through high waters of hell to get her or get to her, he values whatever it is about her that sets off his thermostat of romance and love. It doesn't matter who else is in the running (with the exception of marriage). He aims to come out on top, with dignity of course.

No well-established, respectful, hardworking career woman wants to be with a man who doesn't respect what she has going on and respect her as a woman. So, he has to be on his game.

You must find out what you can about her (if you don't know already) from creditable people. The reason being is so you can have something to talk about should you get the chance to be in her presence. Gentlemen, if you are unable to obtain any information about her, test the waters lightly but don't lose yourself. Women don't care for weaklings.

Now, let's turn the tables, if a woman wants the attention of a man, of course, she thinks her good looks and charms will do it. Plus, that killer walk away rotation of the hips will surely pull a man in – or, at least, get her a stare or a conversation.

Men mostly, if not totally, are visual. So, if your rotating hips are what got his attention, what happens if you slip your hip and start to walk with a limp? What's going to keep his attention? He will need something to keep his vision attentive and sparks flying. This is where most women miss it.

She says, "He has to accept me the way I am,"

Well, that's not what you said when you were trying to get him. What you used to attract his attention is no longer the same. Yes, time brings about a change. But, he needs an alternative. And, if she's smart this second chance or this time around, she'll choose something that's more grounded and consistent that will stay in place for the duration of their marriage or as long as possible.

That hip rotating used to work on all men. But, nowadays, men are asking about a woman's credit score. Yes, you heard me right. It's time for men to realize that, if you were focused and disciplined enough to get your business in order, then, when you bring another person into your life that's one of the questions should be asked before proceeding to the next level and let that determine where you go from there.

Oh, and one more thing, fellows, stop telling a woman everything you can do for her and all you have to offer before getting to know her and what it is she's looking for. Yes, you can be just as cautious and picky with who you give your love, money and time to as well.

Too many men allow the human chicken syndrome to direct their relationships. You know, the two breasts, two legs, and two thighs. Chickens are good, but how about that eagle mentality. Yes, they have the same general parts. But, their direction is different and they don't land the same.

A chicken is possibly airborne for a few seconds. Then, it's back on the ground. But, the eagle sores with the wind beneath its wings. They choose where to land because they have a higher view of sight. Therefore, there are more choices.

There are some men that will choose the chicken, and that's okay because it can be a pleasure in several ways. If he's well-established and there's potential there, then they can grow together and move forward toward desires. So can the eagle, just in larger portions. Don't expect eagle-like mentality from a chicken's perspective. It all depends on the bigger picture.

All I'm saying is choose wisely with your mind's eye. Don't rely on your heart because it changes and it's untamable. I challenge you to read what The Good Book has to say about the heart of mankind. We can't handle it, but God can.

Before Frankie went to Náyai's office, he dashed home to clean up so his first impression in years would be a good one. *Will she be excited to see me?* He thought, *Will she even remember who I am and that we shared so many close romantic encounters in high school? Will she remember me and rush into my arms, and tell me she's been looking for me too?* It was all wishful thinking.

Frankie arrived at Náyai's job around lunch time, hoping to get the chance to take her to lunch and catch up on old times. When he got there, Náyai was in a meeting that would be over shortly. Frankie decided to wait for her. The receptionist kept staring at him as if she thought she knew who he was or had seen him before.

When Mr. Wymey decided to give Súanvier to Frankie, he took him to a lot of black-tie functions where Frankie met a lot of people, got the chance to see how the restaurant industry works, and how to make it successful. *Perhaps, that's where she may have seen me. Or, maybe the cruise?* It didn't matter to Frankie though. The only woman he was interested in was in a meeting and soon would be face to face with him.

Showing up unannounced wasn't the best action to take. But with everything that has happened in his life up to this point, it was worth taking a chance. When the meeting was over, the staring receptionist buzzed Náyai and informed her she had a guest who has been waiting for her.

She whispered, "He's good looking too."

This piqued Náyai's attention. So, she freshened her make-up and lip stick (because that's important) before she walked out into the receptionist foyer. Her expression when she saw Frankie confirmed she remembered their time together long ago. Frankie stood up and greeted Náyai with a warm hug. She invited him into her office, and they started to talk about their careers and future plans to help the less fortunate.

Frankie invited Náyai to Súanvier for lunch, where she was very impressed with his choice of venue. *This is a very expensive place*, she thought to herself. Not knowing Frankie was the owner, she noted, *He's really serving up a great first impression.* Not wanting her to know just yet he owned the restaurant, Frankie walked up to his host with his eyebrows raised to alert him not to give him away as his boss but to treat him as a regular dinning guest. The host understood Frankie's gesture and didn't give him away. The host made sure that the staff knew to do the same too.

Frankie whispered to Náyai she could order anything she wanted and that he knew the owner. She smiled at his comment and thanked him. After they ordered, they continued to talk about careers and future plans. She shared how she wanted to be a nurse so she could somehow be a help to those who were less fortunate or needed some type of medical assistance.

With a puzzled look Frankie asked, "Why didn't you pursue it? What changed your mind to become a social worker?"

"I couldn't afford the tuition at the time so, becoming a social worker was doable and I really like it," she said.

"If you got the chance to go to nursing school, would you still be interested?" He asked with a pleasant smile and raised eyebrow.

"Maybe, but I'm not sure if time is on my side," she admitted.

"What do you mean about time?"

"Well, that was years ago and I'm a lot older now. There are other things I want to do with my life, and school can be very time consuming. It was very important to me then but, once I became a social worker, I find it just as rewarding."

"Okay, so where do you go from here?" Frankie asked, hoping there was room for him in her life somewhere.

"Well I haven't did much traveling, seeing the world. I've always wanted to travel just a little. I don't want my life to be all work and no adventure. So, we decided to take a Caribbean Cruise."

Frankie heart dropped when she said "we." The first thought that came to mind was, *She has a man in her life,* and once again fate has dealt him a bad hand. She noticed his expression changed and he became very silent. Guessing she knew what was going through his mind, she didn't give him a way out. *If he wants to know if "we" meant I was going with a lover or a friend, he would have to be inquisitive enough to ask.*

It was time for Náyai to get back to work. They got up and he walked toward the door. She turned and looked at him as if to say, "Aren't you going to pay the bill?"

He smiled and repeated, "I told you I know the owner."

She smiled and he walked her back to her office. It was a long quite walk. He wanted to ask her if she was in a relationship but felt it may be inappropriate or too soon. *And, what if she said yes.* They made it back to her office. As they said their goodbyes and he got up to leave, he thanked her for letting him take her to lunch, She had an ask-me look on her face, but Frankie was so focused on what she said earlier until he didn't pay attention to her expression.

Before he walked out the door, he turned and asked in a nervous voice, "Are you seeing anyone?"

She replied, "I thought you'd never ask. No, not anymore."

His heart started beating triple time. He asked her if he could see her again. She handed him her business card.

"Call anytime," Náyai said.

Frankie said, "Okay," and left.

For the first time in a long time, things seemed to be going in his favor. He couldn't believe the woman of his dreams, his high school love, was unwedded and single. After pouring himself a glass of wine, he sat and thought about how close he came to missing out on one of the best moments ever by assuming she had someone already.

NEWS FLASH

Some men will possibly talk themselves out of a relationship, or won't approach a woman for a few reasons:

1. Past hurt
2. Low male esteem (that's in the "Jonesanary" dictionary)
3. Lack of confidence
4. Feeling he's out of his league
5. Not financially stable
6. Believing society's lies

Fellows, if you're bold enough to walk up to her or step in her presence, then give yourself the opportunity to change history or make new memories.

The picture or persona you see isn't always what it is. What I mean by that is she may appear to look out of your league. You may be going off of what society has taught you to believe (bougie or high maintenance).

The vast majority of us women love to look good when we step out into the public. So, what you could be seeing is a well-dressed, confident, balanced woman with adequate self-esteem. Only you know the type of woman you desire. Don't approach her if you're half convinced that you want to try.

My multiplication is a half thought, half stable, half confident man is mostly looking for that caliber of a woman – even though he can reach higher if desired, and the same for her. But, a 100% well-established, mannerable, disciplined, chivalrous gentleman is looking for that level of woman. He could even desire someone who's slightly different, but not less. If anything, more than that.

Just like a woman, when she gets her feet planted solid and firmly on the ground (meaning she's established and or is in a better place in life), a man has the right to be just as picky and cautious because of his accomplishment as well. Does one work harder than the other to find the right mate, lover or spouse? I don't think so.

In my opinion, you only work as hard as the level of ladder you choose to climb. The questions here are: How high do you want to go? How far are you willing to climb to balance out your hard-working desires for a long-lasting love or relationship, or even marriage?

What I have learned and observed about men is they say more in silence than in spoken words, which is the opposite of women. The more we pay attention to our man (or men period), the more absorption of their ways we will become aware of. You ever wonder why, when there's a one-way heated conversation going on, he's not participating and shut down communicating? It's because it's not his nature and he knows whatever he says won't be heard or understood most of the time.

It would be like trying to use a microphone that's unplugged. Nothing is getting through, so *nothing is heard. Or, like a car fully fueled with the engine roaring, but there's no motor oil in it. It will eventually throw a rod and kill the motor.*

Most of the time, men are expected to hush, remain silent, take it up the tailpipe, and follow given instructions on the "Honey To Do List" and all the other duties asked and expected. Then, if all isn't done, he's put in the YDG Zone (You Don't Get). So, when respect shows up with an open heart and a set of listening ears, your "To Do List" may, or may not, be finished. But, the YDG Zone may be welcomed. You'll figure that one out by Friday night, or Saturday morning when he comes in.

A few days had passed and Frankie was on top of the world, until he got a phone call from Eboni and Ivory wanting to hook up again. He had forgotten about the cruise rendezvous. He was trying to figure out how they knew where to find him. Was his luck starting to change? Was fate turning the tables on him because of a one-night stand menajahtwa? Frankie figured if he ignored them then, perhaps, they would go away. So, he didn't respond to their invitation.

Náyai was in another one of her regular weekly meetings, but couldn't concentrate. She kept thinking about Frankie -aka- Franklin D. Deluvirus. She thought about how he has really made his life a life of fulfilled desires for himself. Knowing the conditions he grew up in, she was happy for him. She was also surprised she was just as infatuated with him now as she was in high school.

Could love be in the cards for them? Seeing as to how they never dated, Náyai knew that's what Frankie wanted. And, to her, it was a possibility. However, they would have to get to know one another on a personal basis again and see if adulthood agrees with them being in a serious relationship together. She knew she had to pace herself.

Frankie finished going over the books of all his restaurants and wanted to call Náyai and invite her out on a date to get things started between them until he found some discrepancies at The Topaz-Château-Blee. The books showed one amount, but the deposit slips to the bank showed something else. He hired an investigator. Soon, Frankie found out a couple of his bookkeepers were attempting to embezzle money from him. They were unable to cover their tracks because the system was set up to alert Frankie, even on the smallest mistake.

Each restaurant is set to average a certain amount of cash each night, according to its capacity. The money is deposited and notification is sent to Frankie's phone. It was two employees he gave a chance to prove themselves like it was given to him, remembering someone gave him a chance (overlooking the environment he was raised in and the fact he had little to no experience). They failed in taking the opportunity to excel, so he was forced to let them both go. Stealing from him meant they couldn't be trusted.

Not sure if he was still in the mood to go out, Frankie poured himself a glass of wine and started to think. *Would she pick up on my bad mood? Or, would I not be as attentive as I need to be, trying to make a good impression? Should I just call it a day and wait for a better time? Anyway.*

Frankie was down two bookkeepers and needed to replace them as soon as possible. Deciding to wait, he called Mr. Wymey and told him what happened and asked where he could find two trusting bookkeepers. Mr. Wymey reminded him of

Horatius, one of the bartenders who has a background in management and finances.

"He didn't care about the position. He just wanted to work at one of the most eloquent restaurants on the Northside, The Topaz-Château-Blee," Mr. Wymey said.

"It would mean a raise and promotion. He has proven to be a loyal, prompt, customer-friendly, respectful employee," Frankie said.

Frankie decided to meet with Horatius to see if he would be interested in the promotion. Horatius gracefully took the new position and assured Frankie he wouldn't regret it. Now, he only needed one more bookkeeper and it would be business back to its usual status. Frankie was into giving others a chance to move up and move forward in their career and/or life. So, he went back to his hometown and checked with his old high school principal to see if he had any recommendations for filling the opening at The Topaz-Château-Blee.

Mr. Johnson was delighted Frankie remembered the most important moto, "When you make it (if you're in position to do so) go back and help someone else." Gee Gee aka Tritisha, Mr. Johnson's oldest daughter, was the perfect person for the position. She got off to a bad start after high school, went to college and made a few bad choices, but nothing that landed her behind bars or tainted her record. It was a lesson well learned on how not to take education for granted and that great opportunities don't usually knock twice in a lifetime. But, fate was on her side. After getting it together, Tritisha decided to study Law and Finance.

"An impressive background and just the woman for the job, if she's interested though," Frankie told Mr. Johnson.

He set up a meeting with Tritisha and informed Mr. Johnson she would have to prove herself. He told him there would be no favoritism and no second chances in this particular position. Mr. Johnson agreed and respected Frankie for being a shrewd businessman, able to separate business from friendship and acquaintances.

Tritisha took the position and was excited to finally be able to spread her wings and leave the nest (her hometown). She and Horatius worked well together, and The Topaz-Château-Blee was back in stride again and on track. Surely, the favor of the higher powers was on his side. Life was a rollercoaster, but the ups seemed to be longer than the downs.

Now, only if he could find his mother his heart would be more peaceful. Frankie called the investors and they still hadn't been able to find his mother. However, they did have a small lead.

"She was seen a few days ago on the street you grew up on, in an old abandon house," the lead investigator said.

It broke Frankie's heart to get that news and have to accept that she disappeared on him. But, it was better news than no news at all. Frankie was faithful she was still alive. He knew deep down that it was just a matter of time before he found her and could share his good life with her.

It had been a long week, and Frankie hadn't called or heard from Náyai. He was so occupied trying to find replacements for The Topaz-Château-Blee he forgot about his plans to ask Náyai out to dinner. He called and got her voicemail. He left a message asking her to call him when she had time. He dared not ask her out on a date via voicemail.

NEWS FLASH

It's never wise or polite to ask a woman out on a date via text or email. It's distasteful, ungentlemanly like, and women with standards won't go for it.

Now, what is forgotten most of the time by women with a working successful man, life happens and intended things are forgotten and are put on the back burner. Meaning, what was important to you at that time in the moment was interrupted by something more pressing that needed to be taken care of expeditiously. This action will cause a man to be ridiculed and labeled with unkind name calling. But, it's understood for a woman. Talk about double standards! Here's one that's seldom noticed, if mentioned at all.

Do understand, I'm not female nor male bashing. It's just that society would have you to believe that only men display and have double standards or double-minded ways and thoughts. But, as you can see, that isn't true. We all, most of the time, want what we want and when we want it. And, if splitting hairs is the way to get it, as creatures of wants and habits, we go for it.

After feeling so accomplished, Frankie began to reminisce on how he got to this point in his life and how hard it was not being able to share it with his mother. Even though she didn't believe in his dream, it meant a lot to him and would give him so much peace to find her and make sure she's well taken care of.

After a few days, Náyai called and Frankie invited her out on an official date. Since dinner and a movie were such a norm for all new dates, he decided to take her to a secluded hilltop where they could have a nice talk while looking over the city at night lights during the sunset. If she wanted to have dinner later, then he would take her to the place of her choice.

It is so nice to be in the company of a woman who didn't have a lot of dating expectations and ritual habits, he thought to himself. Being able to go with something different and out of the dating ordinary was breathtaking to him. Not to mention, he was with the one woman he'd dreamed of impressing for years.

Náyai had a plan of her own that didn't involve being around a lot of people, just the two of them and a wrapped basket of goodies and wine for two. She told Frankie she had something for him when he picked her up. But, he had no idea she was going to suggest a quiet place for two.

Before she could ask, Frankie told her he wanted to take her to a place a little different from the normal dinner and a movie date. Náyai smiled and felt they were, *perhaps*, on the same page. Once they were on the hilltop, they sat and started to talk about how life had been for them and all the dreams and desires they had for the future.

Frankie was so excited to be in a great place in his life, and with the prettiest woman in the world. He's been bitten by the love bug. The longer they sat and talked, the more he wanted to kiss her. He didn't want to be presumptuous, so he followed her lead. Náyai told him that it was time to take the night to the next level. Frankie smiled and started to lean in for their first kiss. He was stopped with her finger against his lips.

She whispered, "Not yet."

She gave him a little peck on the cheek to save his pride. They enjoyed the goodies and wine, and discussed their future together – where they wanted to go from here, dreams, desires, hopes, family and friends. Frankie wasn't ready to tell her about the situation with his mother yet. He figured he'd wait for a better time (if there was such a time). He didn't want to put a damper on the night when it appeared to be so promising.

Náyai had never met Frankie's mother and he never talked about her to anyone. He knew sooner or later the subject would come up. He figured *later* and decided he'd cross that bridge when he came to it. Procrastination wasn't his mentality, but the night was special. He just wanted to bask in it as long as it lasted without having to feel melancholy about the situation with his mom.

It was getting late and their date night was ending. They packed up everything and headed to the car. Before he could get the basket in the car, Náyai grabbed him from behind – giving him a hug while resting her head on his back and thanking him for a lovely evening. A warm streak flashed through him and he became very excited. It wasn't quite the way he imagined the hug would take place, but he would take it any way he could get it.

It took Frankie by surprise. So much so until he pitched the basket in the back seat and quickly turned to reciprocate the affection, nearly knocking Náyai down. He caught her around her waist and drew her in close. It was a moment to remember. And, the perfect time for that long-anticipated kiss he has been waiting on. Their eyes meet for permission and it happened.

All of his memories and desires rushed through his mind and his body. The proof was obvious. She realized their excitement needed to be a bit more private, so she suggested to end the night at her place. Once they arrived at Náyai's condo, Frankie declined and told her they should wait.

He said he wanted to make sure their time together was not just a heated moment of horniness and infatuation. He thought about the cruise catastrophe with Eboni and Ivory. It wasn't all bad, but he had to make sure making love to Náyai wasn't just a casual act. He wanted her to know this part of his life was just as important as the journey he'd travel to reach every goal so far.

Did he want her? Of course, but he had to think with more than his lower region. It was too big of a chance to take for granted. Náyai was a little confused but appreciated Frankie's reason and called it a night. Lying in her bed, she began to think about the date and checked herself out to see if there was something she could have done differently that would have enabled her to wake up with him the next morning.

Or, at least share an even more intimate night together. Nothing came to mind. But, it still made her wonder. *I guess getting to know him is going to be just as different and our first date was. This is nothing I'm use to or have ever experienced with any guy I've dated, and I like it,* she thought to herself.

NEWS FLASH

I know that it sounds unrealistic for a man to decline sex. Just remember, fellas, just because clichés and society says or believes NO man would turn it down, that doesn't mean it hasn't happened. Don't allow your decency and respect to be hidden or go unnoticed! You too have a choice to choose who to give your love to. Just because she's the love and desire of your life, that doesn't automatically make you hers.

Just because a woman decides to be sexually intimate, that doesn't mean she's in it for the long haul. These days and time aren't like they use to be. Old, antiquated dating and relationships have sailed further out to sea, and only a little of those ways are still around. Believe it or not, you have just as many women loving sex as men. A man may have a different way of going about getting it, but we women also need to know that he's still interested and that we're the only one he's giving it to. To get what we want by increasing the pleasure, put your claws up, ladies.

I'm just keeping it real. The highest level of respect during their date was him deciding not to sleep with her. It made her think and check herself. It made her realize he was different. It was her first no to sex. She didn't control the intimacy with her response, and she liked it.

Fellas, it's good when you can cause a woman to stop and see things through a different set of eyes. It's also good when you show her that you have a choice too when it comes to who you want to give your loving to and why.

Náyai was in one of her morning meetings but couldn't focus. She kept thinking about last night and what didn't happen. Frankie had called her to say good morning and check to see if everything was still a green light with their agreeing to date and continue getting to know one another. She was very delighted he called. It started her day off with hope and a smile.

On the other hand, Frankie was worried Náyai would think badly of him and think he didn't want to sleep with her – which couldn't be furthest from the truth. She was special and he wanted her to not only think it but know it. Nothing was too good for her. There was nothing he would do to cheapen her, including sleeping with her on their first date.

He remembered hearing his mom say, "Things you value, you tend to invest a lot of time and money in. And, when it's a person, the value increases."

The week was a good one, he was glad Náyai was on board and she felt like this part of life with Frankie was what she needed, what had been missing. She hadn't told him just how she felt about him and how impressed she was with their first date. But, after the dozen of purple long-stem velvet roses and an edible floral arrangement was sent to her office during the week, it was definitely time to reciprocate the love and sweet gestures.

After realizing how serious Frankie was about intimacy, Náyai put on her female intuition cap and planned a nice weekend. After calling to check Frankie's schedule, she made a few calls and the weekend was a go. She rented a loft in a secluded bed and breakfast area for the weekend and ordered strawberries and vintage wine. She got to the loft to prepare the place, and had a car sent to pick him up at seven o'clock.

Yes, Frankie was impressed and excited to see what respecting her as the woman of his dreams would get him. Not a game, just respecting what he valued. Unbeknownst to Náyai, Frankie decided to use his own car because he had a few plans of his own. He paid the driver Náyai sent for him and excused him for the rest of the day.

The week prior, Frankie leveled up and bought himself a luxury car. It was time he started to enjoy life as the millionaire he was, and the cream on top of his pie was Náyai. The weekend went as planned. They enjoyed one another. They had glass shattering, diamond cutting, mind blowing, ice melting, sexual healing, sex, breakfast, dinner and more sex. What more could one ask for after months of dating and anticipating?

Months has passed and it was time Frankie told Náyai all about his life, the present and the past. All she knew was he owned two restaurants, lived uptown in the Jonesy D. Regalia Penthouse, and drove a G35. Their romantic weekend getaway she found out everything after he drove up in his 62S Maybach Landaulet Mercedes that was driven by his own chauffer. Needless to say, Náyai was not only impressed but was, again, confused about his life and what else he hadn't shared with her.

On their way back, Frankie began to share that he was the owner of seven restaurants. He explained them all in detail to her. He told her they were:

1. Suanvier – A restaurant for the rich and famous and all who desired to dine in;

2. Topaz Chateau Blee – The restaurant that served international entrees of all kinds;

3. Sylvery Moon – The lovers' nest with low lights that's open late in the evening right before the sunset. This is where marriage

proposals happen, and meet-and-greet couples come mostly to make history. Once a couple came back to take their bridle pictures here, the place where the proposal took place;

4. The Purple River – When the sun sets on this bayside restaurant, the closest body of water is purple. And, when it's a full moon, the scenery is breathtaking;

5. Mon Plaisir (My Pleasure) – The restaurant where you can have it the way you want it. Your dinner is prepared right in front of you, just the way you like. It is a pleasure to accommodate your appetite and desire;

6. Platinum – The restaurant that's platinum through and through. Dress code is enforced, evening gowns and black-tie attire required, and reservations are mandatory. Political, business and charity fundraising events are held here; and,

7. Lady Mable's Kitchen – The restaurant that was named for Frankie mother, whom he

wants to head and run it (with all the profits to be hers). It was purchased with her in mind. Down-home cooking with healthy choices as well, it is fully staffed and just waiting on its rightful owner, Ms. Mable. Until then, Ms. Eubanks is acting interim Supervisor.

Then, Frankie finally told Náyai about the search for his mother. He told her how he went back for her but, once he told her about his new life, she disappeared.

"Investigators are looking for her," he informed.

Frankie always got a little melancholy when he talked about finding his mom. Náyai noticed the mood change. She immediately kissed him and agreed to use her office to help find Ms. Mable. Frankie's face lit up. Life as he desired it had begun. He turned and asked Náyai if she would be interested in them dating exclusively, and she said yes.

"But, not because of your status," she said, "Because you make me feel like I'm the only woman for you, and that has never happened to me, ever."

Frankie told Náyai he knew her loyalty and her feelings were true because she allowed him to share his passion with her before she knew everything about his financial status. He felt she was in it from the heart. The night ended with him dropping her off at home. Afterwards, he received a call from the investigators. They said there was no new news about his mother.

Their week started with the same routine. She was in meetings and he was checking the books of the restaurants and his emails for the day. With the new romance in his life, Frankie started looking for a more permanent place of residence. It was time to prepare for more than just himself. He just had one more bridge to cross.

He hoped and prayed that Náyai would be on board with his mother living with them. Yes, he had plans to ask Náyai for her hand in marriage, while fate was being extra good to him and working in his favor.

The evening ended and Náyai had turned in for the night. So did Frankie, so he thought. His phone rang. It was Tritisha. She wanted to know if she could meet with him on tomorrow.

"Of course," Frankie said. "Is everything alright?"

"Things couldn't BE BETTER," Tritisha said, with emphasis.

"I'll meet you in my office at 10 a.m.," he said.

"Yes, sir," she responded and hung up.

Frankie had no idea what Tritisha wanted, since she had proven to be very good at her job. Tritisha was young, beautiful and smart. Not to mention, she won every pageant she ever entered. She really is a knock-out kind of woman. And, her father was very proud of her for turning her life around and focusing on her career.

Tritisha was a year behind Frankie and Náyai in high school, but her reputation preceded her. She was wild but intelligent, creative and innovative. She influenced those around her, and she was a bit presumptuous. Most of her ways was due to her father being the principal of the school.

It was morning and Tritisha was waiting on Frankie. When he arrived at his Topaz Château Blee office, she smiled as he walked through the foyer.

"Good morning, Tritisha, give me a minute," Frankie said. "I'll be with you momentarily."

Tritisha sat patiently waiting. Thoughts were racing through her head, wondering if this would be the meeting to change her life. Guinevere, Frankie's executive assistant, told Tritisha Frankie was ready to see her. With a bold smile and a sashay stroll, she walked in his office, closed the door, and locked it. Frankie was a bit confused by her actions, until she started to unbutton her blouse.

NEWS FLASH

A man's happiness can be referred to by what he sees and thinks is a better path in life to take.

As unfair as you may think it is that women have to seal the deal of love when it comes to wanting a long-term relationship and or marriage, we have been told that it's the man that has to make her feel secure in a relationship.

Well, let's take a look at how that's been working so far. Since we know that all males have egos, I have observed that they feel its attached to the better part of themselves and to their description whether they're a father, uncle, brother, husband etc., it's never going away.

So, yes, they walk by sight. But, that doesn't mean they don't have a heart of love or loyalty to give. It just means give them something that's real and true to see. They won't have to guess and gather their own thoughts of who, what, when, where and why. Let's continue this in the sequel to **IT'S A MAN'S WORK THAT'S NEVER DONE, NOT A WOMAN'S**.

ACKNOWLEDGEMENTS

I am monumentally grateful to God for giving me this topic, and for the manifestation of this book. I am grateful for the Holy Spirit in my life, and the lessons I've obtained.

Though there have been higher ladders to climb and moving mountains to speak to, this journey is well worth it.

I thank my children, family and friends for their love and support.

I would also like to thank the elders in my life for sharing with me what the path of life could be, with endurance and determination and what it has to offer.

Most importantly, I thank each reader for taking the time to read my book and let my words enhance and balance your life, if I may. Please don't hesitate to reach out to me should you choose to share your thoughts.

Thank You!

THE ART & ARTIST

THE BOOK

Published with assistance from BePublished.org in November 2019, **IT'S A MAN'S WORK THAT'S NEVER DONE, NOT A WOMAN'S** is the debut literary release by Texas author Shirley A. Jones. This candid take on the life of men from the perspective of a woman who loves and knows them well is a controversial yet unifying offering that is sure to keep you glued to each sentence.

"The world (men and women) mostly caters to teaching, showing and informing women how to choose a good man, how to catch a good man, how to tell if he's real, true, honest, loyal etc. There's an enormous amount of books and movies that assist these actions and that's okay. But, who's informing and assisting the men we say we want (loyal, trustworthy, helpful, loving, honest etc.) with how to?" The author observes. "It's okay to express to him how you like what you like and what works for you, what will enhance your love, kindness, loyalty, honesty, truth and trust WITHOUT a hidden agenda. What I mean is don't forget you shouldn't be the only one receiving."

Shirley advises: "Whatever it is that you want, you should be willing to reciprocate. There's no duplicate of who you are. Don't make him guess. Express. I challenge you to read the book and see how the status of a man doesn't keep him from doing what he needs to do, and how to get the most out of loving and respecting him. Just know, he too can be just as picky about who he gives his love to. As you will read, these three scenarios will show different perspectives on how IT'S A MAN'S WORK THAT'S NEVER DONE, NOT A WOMAN'S."

Available as an ebook for $9.95, **IT'S A MAN'S WORK THAT'S NEVER DONE, NOT A WOMAN'S** by Shirley A. Jones may also be purchased worldwide as a paperback for $19.95 from bricks-and-mortar and online book retailers including your local bookstore, Barnes & Noble, Borders, Amazon, and www.ShirleyJones.webs.com.

THE AUTHOR

Shirley A. Jones is a Texas native and longtime Arlington resident. A healthcare industry specialist and proud mother of three, she has volunteered with multiple community organizations and is a spiritual / events / motivational speaker. Singing and writing are fashionable passions that have now been established.

Shirley is also a highly-sought-after performer, frequently asked to perform for private parties and public events. Soon, she will release her first music single in 2020. And, Shirley plans to release other books and organize a book tour around her literary debut, **IT'S A MAN'S WORK THAT'S NEVER DONE, NOT A WOMAN'S**.

www.ShirleyJones.webs.com